THE ANGELS ARE WATCHING

KEKA SAMUELS-WILSON

The Angels Are Watching. Copyright 2024 by Nayo "Keka" Samuels-Wilson. All rights reserved. No part of this publication may be reproduced, distributed, or transmitted in any form or by any means, including photocopying, recording, or other electronic or mechanical methods, without the prior written permission of the publisher, except in the case of brief quotations embodied in critical reviews and certain other noncommercial uses permitted by copyright law.

For permission requests, write to the publisher, addressed "Attention: Permissions Coordinator," 205 N. Michigan Avenue, Suite #810, Chicago, IL 60601. 13th & Joan books may be purchased for educational, business or sales promotional use. For information, please email the Sales Department at sales@13thandjoan.com.

Printed in the U. S. A.

First Printing, September 2024.

Library of Congress Cataloging-in-Publication Data has been applied for.

ISBN: 978-1-953156-90-7

CONTENTS

Dedication iv
Acknowledgements vi
To My Readers xi
Disclaimer xiii
1. Teen Runaway 1
2. Wildin' In The Streets 7
3. Narrow Escape 12
4. A Hard Bluff 20
5. Surviving Depression 24
6. Domestic Violence
   Arrest 29
7. Nervous Breakdown 33
8. Rape 38
9. Crack Addiction 45
10. The Bahamas 77
11. Child Protective
    Services 92
12. Apartment Robbed 100
13. Roofie 113
14. Family Sponsor 118
15. Sisters With Angelic
    Wings 123
16. Joined The Army 136
17. Upstate Arrest 143
18. NYPD Raid 148
19. Yacht Party 158
20. Finding Jesus 164
21. The Transition 186
22. My Pain for His Glory ... 202
Lesson I Learned Overall ... 210
Salvation Prayer 215
Gospel Playlist 217
Devotionals 220
The Great Commission 232
Resources 233

DEDICATION

This book is solely dedicated to You God, my Heavenly Father, Hallowed be thy name!
No earthly being can share this spot with You.
Nothing is done by accident from You God! So if nothing is done by accident and all is done by Your divine purpose, then I thank You for all the trauma and hardships I had to go through to become who I am today.

My Prayer:

Dear God, I just want to thank You for Your endless love for me. You were there for me far before I knew of You or even thought of coming to You. I will forever thank You for Your precious act of everlasting and unconditional love, where You sent down Your Son, Jesus, for my redemption and salvation, so that I could be a part of You again.

Thank You for Your love and patience to give me chance after chance to get it right and for choosing me to fulfill this assignment for You, Your people, and the "widows" of this world. For this is Your book, and I'm

Dedication

just Your messenger. I am ready to serve! I have been changed from the inside out and will spend the rest of my days making You known.

Lastly, thank You for sending Your angels down to guard and watch over my children, my family, and me. I love You and give You all the Praise, the Honor, and the Glory. For You are more than worthy. May Your Will be done and this book bring others to Christ.

I love You!
Amen.

ACKNOWLEDGEMENTS

Mom and Dad. Brenda and the late Rev. Robert E. Samuels. My love to you both for bringing me into this world and teaching me the ways of the Lord so that when I departed, I knew how to find my way back to Christ, like the prodigal son.

You not only introduced me to God but to a prayer life without me even knowing the power of prayer, just doing it out of obedience to you both. Looking back, I see prayers got me out of a lot of bad situations and definitely into some good ones. And for the times I didn't know how to pray or what to pray, I thank you both for never ceasing to pray for me. Your prayers have covered me and kept me safe throughout my life. The anointing and favor you both have over your lives definitely covered not only me but our whole Samuels family–your children, grandchildren, great-grandchildren, and all the generations to come from you.

Mommy, mommy, mommy. My dear loving mother...thank you for never giving up on me, for loving me unconditionally, even after all the chaos (to put it lightly) that I put you through. And because you never ceased praying after daddy was gone, even up until now, I am still alive today by the Grace of God! Thank you mommy.

Acknowledgements

My Dear Children. All four of you. To my oldest three, Elijah, Nia, and Demitri (DJ), who went through most of my life stories with me, where do I begin? Thank you for never judging mommy and always loving me the same.

No matter what I did, you all still loved me, even when I didn't know what I was doing as I was still raising myself and trying to find my place in life while running the streets with the three of y'all attached to my hip. We had some hard times but because of you all, I never gave up being the best mother I knew to be and strived to become better for you. Again, this time publicly, I give you my apologies for everything I had you witness and go through with me in life. It must've been hard on you when you were so young. May you heal from my mistakes and anything that has impacted you in a negative way and be a better person than I was. May the generational curses be stopped with me and grace continue to cover you all. I made sure I provided for you and protected you. But the one job God had required of me, I failed at. I didn't teach you the ways of the Lord as I should have. May you turn your own lives to Christ. It's not too late for you all. For the longest time I told y'all, "It's the three of us against the world." But all along it was four. I had left God out.

And then you entered my life, Sage. You've shown me that Autism is just a word. I've grown to learn patience while raising you on the spectrum. Thank you for giving mommy the chance to get it right this time. You've given me the chance to raise a child now while I'm wiser and making better choices. May I raise you with God and Christ in your life.

My Hearts. My children; my granddaughter Sanai and grandson Zaire; my nieces Jaemani, Mi'Leah, Jazmyn, Ty'Lee; and nephew Jaylen. May you all continue to follow God and keep growing in Christ. I love you all.

And of Course... Love to my three younger siblings, George, Jamin, and Vanessa. Thank you for always having my back and treating my kids as your own. Yayyy to uncles and aunties! P.S. I spared everyone the home stories when we were younger, since y'all agreed I terrorized y'all as kids, something I definitely don't remember. I had a different perspective than y'all, lol. But we have our own wild stories from growing up. Lol! Continue to hold down the Samuels' household name. Love you all.

I've met so many good people throughout my lifetime. There are too many to name but for the ones I did, you know why and what part of my journey you played in my life and/or my children's lives. Most of you have been through some of these stories with me and some, your stories didn't make it into this book, but I still want to give **Special Thanks To**: Aunt Rosalind; Mrs. Muhammad; my kid's Grandma Annette and Grandma Iris (and all the grandmothers who cared for and loved on my children and me throughout our lives); my kid's "Auntie" Zakiya; Ms. Bonita; Stan; Ms. Juanita; Ms. Loretta; Mike King; my cousins: Tradean, Jean and the late Michelle; Uncle Wade; the Smith family in Georgia, and the rest of my Samuels and Cromwell family who never judged me and looked out for me whenever they could. Those who have been there for us, you know who you are.

My Day Ones (aka Forever Friends). Thank you for holding me and our friendship down, some for over 40 years now: Jennifer, Tamika, Tracy, Jaime, Tasha, and Regina.

I love you all, as you have been tremendous blessings placed along the journey of my life. There are so many family and friends who have loved on me and supported me. And I pray that along the way, it wasn't always one-sided. I hope to have shown my love right back to you.

Acknowledgements

MY BELOVED HUSBAND. Mr. Adrian Wilson. I never thought good men still existed until I met you. Thank you for knowing my past baggage and still loving me with no regrets. For loving and helping me raise my older children as your own, even holding them down along with my mom during my deployment and all the other times I had to leave for Army training. What would our lives be like without you?

You've shown me true love through my addictions and all. Thank you for your love and support through my schooling and careers that kept me away for many hours and sometimes days, crazy ideas (many unsuccessful businesses), and now ministry where we stand together, and everything in between–including the journey of writing this book.

Thank you for assuring me that no matter what went into this book, you would not be ashamed to still call me your wife. For these are my truths. You accepted them and me. Thank you for being a safe space for me as I recollected a lot from my past and cried many nights with you by my side.

You are an exceptional man, husband, father, and friend, and I am so grateful for you and for growing with me spiritually. May our love for each other and Christ's anointing continue to cover us and our family's lives as we continue to grow our family in ministry together with our children. We are just getting started.

I Love You!

13th & Joan Publishing House. Thank you for believing in my message, encouraging me from day one, and partnering with me to bring my story out and into the world. May God bless this book to do more than we could ever ask or imagine.

Sameer Sood aka Digital Creator. Thank you and your team for the hard work and dedication as our graphic designer, social media and website designer, and promoter to help set this book up for the world. https://www.designerfromhills.com

All My Readers. From the bottom of my heart, I want to acknowledge and thank each of you. Many of you wanted to share in my book journey before it was even published and was still a work in progress. I am more than grateful for your support. May this inspire you to move closer to–and have an intimate and personal relationship with–God and Christ. To be the light to the rest of the world for others to see and want to experience Christ for themselves.

And to all who don't know me well or at all, this book was written as my living testimonies to every single one of you who picked up this book to let you know there is a God. One who surpasses all. My life story was pre-written and no matter what anyone or I tried to do to change the course, the outcome would have been the same. I had more than 200 stories written down about my life, but with prayer and fasting, God told me to only include the following in this book. These stories were consequently hand-picked by God for you to bear witness to. It is no coincidence that **you are reading these very words at this present time.** I am a walking epistle to you. May my words contain messages of consolation to the troubled people, give hope to the righteous, and bring light to the unrighteous to seek Christ. **THIS BOOK, MY DEAR FRIEND, WAS WRITTEN FOR YOU!** So be encouraged and be inspired. You are all loved. Thank you for your love, care, and support in purchasing and reading my book. May this book bless you the way my Father Willed it.

All written with love,
Keka

TO MY READERS

October 2020, I gave my life back to Christ.

December 2020, God told me, "On the other side of that drink is your purpose." I didn't understand then but from that day forward, He took the desire away from me and I quit drinking alcohol for the last time. After 31 years of HARD drinking, with blackouts and passing out all the time, I never drank again.

Not long after December 2020, God told me to write down my stories. I didn't understand my assignment at first. Over time, I realized my stories and testimonies were written to inspire others to know that God will turn their pain into triumph when they turn their life to Him and Christ. During the process of writing, I faced so much resentment and harbored pain in my life. I finally came face-to-face with it all and began to heal without shame or guilt. This book was intended as my own therapy and healing, as well as to minister to you all.

I was very reluctant with this assignment in the beginning. I definitely didn't want my "business" out there. But God started working on my mind, spirit, and soul, and my healing process began. Lots of days and nights of tears and prayers went into writing this book. Like me, just know that God will see you through and turn your pain into purpose when you hand it over to Him. He does not waste your pain. He uses your experiences to help others.

This book is not about me being a victim to the streets all of my life. I don't need a pity party because truthfully, don't we all go through things in life? Don't we all have stories to tell, some worse than others? But these words are my true living testimonies, inspired by God to be written to encourage you. To tell you that God has you surrounded by His angels, whether you believe it or not. But believe me, without His protection, we'd all be worse off and wouldn't have made it past half of our experiences so that we now have stories to tell to help others. This book was also written to inspire you to want to get to know Him better through Christ. By doing that and your obedience to Him, not only will He have an eternal reward waiting for you, but this life-long process we live here on earth will be a more peaceful journey because you'll be able to identify your purpose and live fulfilling it. All you have to do is try Jesus for yourself.

Be encouraged. It's not over for you. It's just the beginning. For now, I finally understand what my assignment was...to tell you to seek Christ for yourself.

DISCLAIMER

I'm not in the business of snitching on anyone. I'm not here for anything more than telling the stories of my truths, as my witness to God's protection provided by Him and His Angel Armies. Few names have been changed or omitted to not shame, guilt, or get anyone in trouble. Actual names that remain are to recognize that person's special love and the care that they've shown my children and me throughout our lives. They were and still are our angels sent to us in human form.

In addition, subject matter such as addiction, depression, rape, etc., have been touched upon in this book. Please be advised that these topics may trigger uncomfortable feelings in some readers.

For he will command his angels concerning you to guard you in all your ways; they will lift you up in their hands... -Psalm 91:11-12 **(NIV)**

TEEN RUNAWAY

The Lord our God is merciful and forgiving, even though we have rebelled against him;

Daniel 9:9 (NIV)

Let me take you back to the beginning. Let me walk you, slowly, through my life of turmoil. I won't start with you from the very beginning, before my elementary school years. Not because I don't have stories that early, but because I have to save something to put in my next book, right? The first time I ran away from home was at 10 years old. Ask me how that went. Not well. I ran away because my younger brother was sick one day during his week of doing dishes, and my mom told me to do them for him that night after dinner. I was mad because he never did my dishes when I was sick. I felt like he was always getting away with more than me. I felt like he was her favorite child. Why did I always have to do everything? So I ran away to my Aunt Rosalind's house, only to get to the subway station around the corner from me. The admission then was token coins. I realized I didn't know what two trains to ride to Harlem from the Bronx and what stops to get off. My mom always took us with her, and I never paid attention. I just followed her lead. So there I was in the station, stumped. I called my aunt from the pay phone at the station, and she asked me why I was traveling without my mom. Needless to say, she knew something was up. I don't remember what I told her. She asked me where I was and said to stay put and she would come to get me. I waited and waited. I saw her coming out of the big fat wooden turnstile, thinking we were going back in to go to her house, but she took me back to my own home. Right back to my mom and dad. Later I learned that as soon as I had hung up with her, she called my mom and found out I was trying to run away and took me right back where I started. Me and my little backpack.

As the years went on, I ran away from home time after time. I always found a reason to be mad and leave again, especially about my curfew as I got older. I was a professional runaway... not even hardly. My "church" parents were strict, and I was tired of their house rules. Of course, all my cousins and friends' homes didn't have as many rules about chores, especially rules about what they were and weren't allowed to do. They also listened to secular music in their homes, and my parents only listened to gospel records. And please, let's not talk about the TV we were limited to watching in my home.

As a teen, especially in my early high school years, I ended up in numerous teen runaway shelters—I always found them through the Yellow Pages —or living on the streets. Not literally on the streets, but meaning the homes of different people or friends from day to day. I even befriended an amazing and kind-hearted woman, who I also found out worked with my dad at a hospital clinic during the day. Mrs. Muhammad. Good ole

Teen Runaway

Mrs. Aqila Muhammad. The "Kwein" is what they call her. Her second, night-time job was at a teen shelter I ended up in one night after searching the Yellow Pages once again. I was in the shelter's office with her doing the intake and she remembered me from visiting my dad at her morning job. From that night on, she took special care of me. There were times I ended up at her apartment door, trying to run away yet again. She would keep me for a night, call my parents, take me home the next day, and sit with us to talk it out, then be on her way again. Whenever I tried to solicit an adult to help me leave home, they took me back to my loving parents. But I will say she did care about me and the youth. I remember she was a foster parent to some babies born to their drug-addicted mothers. I think today she still works as a teacher at the school of the mosque she attends in Harlem. She always cared for me when I was around. That's how I learned about the Nation of Islam and Kwanzaa, which I celebrated with her and her family. And that's when I became more aware of my heritage and culture, wearing my African medallions, Kufis, and such, and became even more proud of my African name that the children made fun of in school. I was a proud Black girl! I learned so much from her. She was the first one I remember asking me how I was doing and meant it. When I said, "*Fine*," She would let me know that wasn't a valid answer and would sit me down and ask how I was really doing and said don't give her any fluff. She really cared about the youth. We stayed in touch throughout the years. I even took my oldest three kids to visit her a few times when I got older. She loved me so much, and I loved her right back. She was a positive influence in my life, especially as a teen runaway. She never judged me, only cared for me. I could never forget her.

So in between the back and forth at the runaway shelters and my home, one day I went to church with my family. That

The Angels Are Watching

was one thing my parents didn't mess with. Whenever I found my way back home, I had to go to Sunday church. When I was younger, it was Sunday, Monday, Tuesday...you get the idea. Sunday schools, Sunday services, children's choir rehearsal, children's usher board rehearsal, adult choir rehearsal and usher board meetings with my parents because they had to attend all their auxiliaries, Bible studies, prayer meetings... all the works. We were in the church almost every single day of the week. But as we were older, we were attending a different church, and I wasn't a part of any organizations. So I was only required to attend Sunday services with my family. This particular Sunday outside after service, a church member turned to me right before she got in her car and asked me, *"How could you do that to your dad?"* I asked, *"Do what?"* She said, *"Do all that stuff to your body."* My dad was a preacher and at that time, I had six piercings in both ears, a nose ring, a lip ring, and colorful (peach-ish) hair with crazy hairstyles. In the 90s, these were all unheard of for little Black girls in the hood. All I could think of was, *"Do this to him??? This is about me and my body. I didn't do anything to him."* But all I said to her was, *"It doesn't bother him."* I thought the nerve of her, especially because she didn't say hi to me or anything. Just being plain rude.

This was also the time I was wearing motorcycle boots in the summer with short shorts and metal belts, etc. People always called me crazy and weird because didn't no Black girls/people from the South Bronx look and dress like that at that time. Only the white kids, downtown in the village, were doing all this. By the way, the village was the spot for me and my girls Jaime and Tasha back then. While everybody stayed on the block, on the corners, or hanging around the bodegas, Jay, Tasha, and I were always downtown in the village. But while they wore what the "Black girls" were wearing, I wore what made me feel comfortable.

Because of all the running away and repeated truancy, I went through three different high schools before I graduated. Graduation only happened with the help of night schools and summer schools. All that and I still ended up graduating a year later than my friends my age. I even had a short stint in a group home in Staten Island during my runaway days while in high school. I was staying at a friend's house. Someone from school snitched and told my mom where I was, and she came and got me. Her and the cops. She had the cops come with her to pick me up as a runaway. The purpose was so they would take me to family court and the judge would send me back home, as a minor, with her. I know now she did it out of her love for me. She was worried about me and my whereabouts because I had been gone for many weeks. At the time, this had been the longest I was gone, so she was worried. They handcuffed me behind my back, I don't know why, and put me in the back of the cop car.

They drove us to the family court in the Bronx on 161st Street. The judge gave me a choice to go back home to my loving parents—he said he could see my mom loved me because why else would she go through this to get me back home—or to a group home because I was underage and could not live on my own without parental supervision. So being the smart a%# that I was, I chose to go to the group home. What did I think going there would accomplish? I ended up in Staten Island, away from everyone and everything I knew. I was across the water and could only see my people on a weekend pass after taking a ferry across the river. I wasn't even allowed to go on the pass until I was there for a certain amount of time, which I never made it to because I was only there about two months. I

The Angels Are Watching

never made it past my probation period. So I was alone in the group home.

My roomie was nice to me, but that wasn't enough. I still had a curfew and chores. Yes, the very things I tried so hard to get away from at home. And the kitchen, dishes, and bathroom were even bigger because they housed so many girls. I was like, *"This ain't life. What was I thinking?"* Then I had the one house mother who seemed nasty and rude. Not loving at all. And when I could finally make a phone call at the allotted time, who was the first person I called? My mom. She asked me how I was doing. Were they treating me well? All I remember was that was all I needed to hear before breaking down. I was crying to her that I didn't want to stay there. I can't remember how much time had passed before my next court date, but when I got back to family court, my Aunt Roz was there with my mom. Yes, that same aunt who years earlier took me back home the first time I tried to run away. My aunt spoke up and said she would take me home with her if allowed. So the judge once again gave me an option. Did he say to return to the group home or live with my aunt??? So I chose to go live in Harlem with my aunt and cousins. That ended my short stint in the group home. I didn't last a year there, not even six months. But being there made me realize that despite all the rules and chores and the freedom I thought I didn't have in my own home, I had so much more.

WILDIN' IN THE STREETS

Surely for my own welfare I had such great anguish;
but Your love has delivered me from the pit of oblivion,
for You have cast all my sins behind Your back.

Isaiah 38:17 (BSB)

What a wild ride my life started out as, including molestation as a younger child in elementary school. That's probably why I became so promiscuous and wild at a young age as I ran with my girls, aka aces, aka best friends Jaime and Tasha. We didn't use the word "bestie" back then. It was us against the world. Us together, always fighting everybody else. Fight after fight after fight. All my life, I had to fight! Fights in school, fights outside of school. Even when I ended up in another high school separate from them, we always played hooky to go to each other's schools and then, we were fighting at all our schools. I was fighting girls because I'm light-skinned and think I'm better than them (their words), fighting cuz their man liked me, fighting cuz I'm short so they thought they could intimidate me, fighting because people just liked to pick a fight with me, lol. I mean I really don't know why I was in half of those fights. But yet and still, there I was. You could catch me in a fight on any given day. One day after cheerleading practice after school, my bamboo earrings were snatched by the projects near Stevenson High School by some guys. My girls and I chased them to get my earrings back. Of course, we never caught them, and I never got them back. But I was willing to fight for them cuz back then, we wore real gold bamboo earrings and jewelry. And my dad had paid for them as a gift to me. When I got a second pair, there was a girl in my school spreading rumors about what she said I had to do, with a guy, to get them again cuz she heard what happened to my first pair. Not even knowing how I got my second pair, so then we had beef. We always tried to fight after school but that never happened, and that's a story for another day.

Jaime, Tasha, and I went through fights on our blocks, other people's blocks, in public places, and in private places. But the fights never started with us. We tried to be good girls. We were mostly fighting because some other girls were "jealous" of us. We used that word instead of hatin' back then. They always started with us while we minded our business just hanging out. Again, they would say I thought I was all that just because I'm light-skinned or because their man liked me, Jaime, or Tasha, even though we stayed away from the guys not to have a conflict with their girlfriends. But they didn't care about all that. Their boyfriends liked us and that was enough to make the girlfriends want to fight and even jump us sometimes. The girlfriends always had beef with us or hated us anyway. I was helping Jaime and Tasha fight their fights, and they helped me fight my fights. We were wildin' back then. I remember some girls from another block came down to my block and jumped me with blades in their mouths over one of the girl's boyfriends I never touched or even talked to or cared about. He liked me but when I gave him no play, he told his girl I was trying to get with him, with me knowing she was his girl. Just lies everywhere. Tasha was around to jump in to help me that time because Tasha and I lived in the same building.

I was fighting for my respect if I wasn't fighting over some guy. Because I'm short, there was so much disrespect toward me on many levels, and yup, I had to prove myself and that lil shorty wasn't no punk. The fights were never-ending, especially during my teenage years. The fight in the welfare office and the White Castle restaurant...Whew! Those definitely were the days. But when I got older and became a mom, then I was always fighting to defend my kids against other kids and especially adults. I didn't play when it came to my kids.

When they were young, my kids always saw me fighting or arguing—in the shelters we lived in, in their schools, in their daycares, in Chuck E Cheese—with other parents, teachers, staff, adults everywhere we went. My whole life was a fight. I promise you I didn't start any of them. People just always picked on me or my kids for whatever reason. I have come a long way. But those teenage years were ruthless. Fighting almost every day for something that was never my fault. Well, that's my story, and I'm sticking to it. I know others may beg to differ. But yeah, for senseless stuff. I can't leave out the fights with the guys I was in relationships with my whole life. All the domestic violence and toxic relationships. With baby daddies and non-baby daddies. So many guys. Yes, I had a lot of those. I picked the same pattern of guys, no matter how hard I tried to find different ones. But like any other fights, some I won, some I lost.

The Angels Are Watching

For many years after realizing the pattern, I wondered why I kept attracting the same type of guys. Was it me? I was not starting physical fights, but perhaps with my mouth? Or my actions? Either way, I never swung the first blow but of course, I ended up having to defend myself every single time, with or without any weapon in sight that I picked up. Just fending for myself, except for the few times I had different guys pull their guns out on me. Then oh yeah, I complied with what I was dealt. It was either that or get ready to die. Those cowards. But then again, I always chose the thugs for such a sweet church girl... Ha! Sweet church girl, I wished. I have enough stories of those I could write a book about. But anyway, in my latter years, once I got tired of fighting in my relationships, I started praying to God to make me a better person and for God to find me a good husband. That's when the narrative changed. But until then, the fights continued. I was fighting everybody everywhere all my life.

Jaime and I were the worst of the three with Tasha. Tasha was always there for the fights but barely went out with us, at all the house parties, drinking 40 ounces of Old E, St. Ides beer, and all the hard liquor as teens, walking down the blocks, drinking out of brown paper bags back then. And let me not forget to mention my first hard liquor drink at 13 was E&J. I mean, guzzling bottles hardcore back then. Not no little sippy sippy like the cute girls did. We were guzzling straight from the bottles like the guys we hung out with, getting into the Tunnel Club at 16 years old, where we met all the celebrities. No ID was required. Meeting up with groups of friends/people in motels, playing strip poker with guys and girls, the jacuzzi parties. Back then, it was called orgies. We were a hot mess, but a hot mess together. All the sex, drugs, and alcohol. Living like rock stars...we were not. We were definitely wildin' in the streets. I definitely was not living the life that my church parents raised me to follow.

As we got in our early 20s, still just mostly me and Jay, still running the streets and clubs every weekend, we were old enough to hit the strip clubs and underground swinger clubs so the escapades were just on a grander scale. Then we really thought we were doing some adult things. Back then, the swinger clubs were so secretive. It was like being amongst the elite. More like the raunchy, X-rated, elite society. You couldn't just walk in off the street and enter these places. It was a whole process back then. You had to sign up through email and get sent back the password to tell at the front door to get in. Very exclusive. Not sure how it's done nowadays. And although we didn't have video recordings on cell phones back then, we did have to hand over our phones with coat check because no pictures were allowed. That would've been invading others' privacy. It would have been a lot for us to witness at that age, but we were professionals by then. I say that jokingly, but we definitely had our share as teens, so we weren't surprised at what we saw there. Maybe different tools and objects used were a little different but for the most part, nothing new to us. We went again and again and again.

One thing I will say about Jaime and Tasha, they never left my side from the beginning of our friendship. On the days I was living in the streets, from friends' homes to friends' homes, runaway shelter to shelter, they always brought me their clothes and food. I was never without. On top of that, Tasha was our hairstylist. She loved doing hair, and I always looked like I had just stepped out of the salon. So although I was homeless a lot as a teen, I didn't look the part as much.

Thank God the promiscuity, fighting, and many of my old ways are over and done with. What I thought was fun was creating my path to my own destruction. Thank God for the forgiveness of my sins.

NARROW ESCAPE

Behold, I give you the authority to trample on serpents and scorpions and over all the power of the enemy, and nothing shall by any means hurt you.

Luke 10:19 (NKJV)

In my late teens when I was closer to graduating high school, I was back from my aunt's place and living with my parents again. I met an older guy named Hasaan in his early 20s, who drove a black BMW. Being naïve, I didn't realize that was what all the drug dealers from the hood drove. I wasn't into dudes with cars just because they were very conceited. That's the word I used back then. He was light-skinned and a little below average height for a guy. He was the total opposite of what I was physically attracted to. Two things I preferred back then were dark-skinned and tall. He was more soft-spoken than most young guys from the hood. He was attentive to me and not as aggressive as most guys I was used to being with. And to drive such a car, he wasn't a flashy or cocky type of guy. How did he get my attention when he was not my type? I don't even know. I don't remember how I met him. I think I was walking down the street and he pulled over, got out to talk, and gave me his number. For a while, I dated him. By dating, I mean us getting drunk and... whatever the phrase was for "Netflix and chill" back then. He never once took me out on a "date."

After seeing each other for about a month or two, he kept asking me to go with him somewhere on a specific school night. I remember because I knew I was trying to have perfect attendance at night school so I could finally graduate after being in my third high school. I was so upset he wasn't taking no for an answer. He kept saying it was only one time, so I relented. Every day, he kept telling me to make sure that when he picked me up by my night school, Roosevelt High School on Fordham Road, to carry an open tote book bag instead of a closed backpack on my back. And to make sure it was empty. And every day, I told him that's the only kind of bag I used for school, and I would have it emptied for him. He was insistent on reminding me every single day. At any rate, it came down to the day, he picked me up by the night school in his car that late afternoon and we drove. I asked questions. *"Where were we going?"* He kept telling me he would explain later but first, he had to see someone and for me to ride with him. So I did.

We drove for a little, parked, and walked about two blocks until we got to an empty Spanish restaurant. I would have thought they were closed because it was empty, but an old Spanish man was sitting at the counter alone. He was the only one I saw. Hasaan and the guy exchanged greetings like they had known each other for a while and had us move to sit at a round table where the customers ate. Hasaan told me to put my bag on the floor, and he slid it under the table with his foot. I still didn't know what was going on. They chit-chatted for a few minutes in Spanish. I had no clue what was being said right in front of me. I was more shocked that my guy knew Spanish. It was choppy and wasn't flowing fluently, but good enough for the other man to understand. Then we got up to leave. Hasaan told me to grab my bag. I noticed a big, yellow manilla envelope in my bag when I picked it up, but didn't question it. I just knew it belonged to him at that point. How, I don't know. But I knew that was why he was stressing me about bringing an open tote bag.

We went outside and got on the bus. The big blue NYC bus!!!??? Then I was asking, *"Why are we going on the bus?"* He said we were going back to his place. I was mad he got me on the bus instead of in his BMW. Funny, cuz I wasn't used to guys with cars. But at that point, he had me spoiled. Picking me up and dropping me off whenever I was with him. So I asked, *"You just gonna leave your car there?"* He said he'd go back to get it later. I never questioned it again. We rode back in silence and when we got to his place, he took his envelope out. It never dawned on me that I was transporting drugs that day. That was the only time he asked me to make a run like that with him. Looking back, I see all the red flags. The open bag was for him to be able to slip the package into it with ease, easier than in a backpack. Of course, going through it, I was young and naive and not hip to the transportation of drugs, although Jaime and I had witnessed the cooking and packaging of drugs at one of her guy's places. That's another story for another day. In hindsight, the scenario played out just like the movies. I never actually saw what was in the envelope, but I say it was drugs because in the beginning of dating, I had asked him where he worked. Of course, he said he didn't. So I asked him how he got the money to buy his car. He told me he sold drugs but never specified which ones, and I didn't put the two together at the time of the transportation. Now I know it had to do with something that had to be cooked on the stove. How do I know? Because of my next story.

The same dude that I did the (unbeknownst to me) drug trafficking with, I hadn't seen for a couple of weeks after that, which was unusual for us. But one day he called me out of the blue and said he wanted to see me. At that point, I was still living back in my parent's home, trying to do the right thing and finish school. He picked me up from there. We went in a different direction than usual to his apartment, so I questioned him, of course. He said he was taking me to a friend's house. We got to a building on the Grand Concourse and went up to a high floor in the elevator. We got to the apartment and he told me to follow him when we entered. I followed him into the kitchen. There was a guy standing over the stove cooking some drugs. Hasaan asked if I knew what he was doing. I said yeah because I remembered seeing it when I ran the streets with Jaime at one of her dude's apartments. So Hasaan told me to follow him some more. We moved on to a bedroom and he pushed me in and locked the door from the outside. Huh? I heard him lock the door. It wasn't pitch black, but it was a little dark inside. The lights were off and the shades were halfway down, but the sun was going down already, so there was not much light. I rattled the doorknob and tried to open it. I started banging on the door with my fists and yelling. Nothing. I looked around the room to see if I could find something to break the door down. I saw two beds. A brown-skinned Black girl was sitting on one with her knees drawn up and arms wrapped around them like a baby up against the corner of the wall. Her bed was partially against the wall and partially against the window, with the shades halfway drawn. She looked close to my age but a little younger.

I didn't realize she was there when I first arrived. So there I went asking questions again. *"What's going on? Why did they lock us in here? What's your name?"* She said absolutely nothing. She looked at me like she wanted to cry, then looked away. I kept asking for her name with no response. I figured she was too scared to talk. But I told her, *"I don't know what you're gonna do, but I'm gonna get us out of here."*

I was thinking and still looking around. Not once did I sit on that other bed. I got an idea. I had on my motorcycle belt and boots. The belt had little spokes on it, not sharp at all, more for design. But it made the belt heavy. I removed it and banged on the door with my fists until Hasaan returned. He returned irate, opened the door, told me to shut the f^&k up, and started hitting me with something metal. I couldn't tell what it was. Maybe a pipe because he could only hit me within arm's reach. I was swinging my belt back. It had more reach, so it kept hitting him more than he was hitting me. Then we fought each other in the doorway. He kept ducking but my belt kept landing on him. I was screaming, *"Let me out."* He finally backed out the door and locked it again from the outside. So there we were again. Me and ole girl. Alone. Now it was pitch black in the room. I looked for a light switch. Found the switch but no light bulb. Nothing. But my eyes adjusted. There was a light post nearby outside that gave us little light under the half-drawn shade. I remember saying to myself, *"Thank God for the light post."* I don't know how I got so much strength to fight that guy, but I'm guessing my adrenaline from fearfulness and wanting to get free gave me strength. I don't know how much time had passed, but he and the other guy came and opened the door and told us they were taking us somewhere. I think I heard the word home. OMG! Home. All I wanted was to get home. I was so confused. I didn't understand what had just happened.

Narrow Escape

Needless to say, the girl and I left the room quietly. We went down in the elevator to the street to a car that wasn't the BMW. I assumed it was the other guy's car because he got in the driver's seat and drove us. He was the driver, Hasaan was in the passenger seat, the girl was behind the driver, and I was behind Hasaan. We drove in silence. I don't know if the guy driving already knew where I lived or if they were talking in the front and Hasaan was giving directions. All I know is I was in my own thoughts, thinking about going home. We literally drove down my block, which was a one-way on Townsend Avenue, and passed my building. I spoke up and said, *"You passed my building."* Hassan told me I was not going home yet. They were gonna take us somewhere else first. I said, *"NO! TAKE ME HOME NOW! I don't want to go nowhere else!"* Every time I looked at the girl, she looked straight ahead and silent. In my head, I'm like, *"F this! I'm getting out of this car."* We drove one block down the street past my building. We stopped at the stoplight. I looked one more time at ole girl. This time she actually looked at me. That was the last time I got a chance to see her face. She actually looked a little younger than me like a scared little girl. I gestured to her door and then to her lock, trying to tell her to unlock her door, but she didn't. I kept thinking we didn't have much time. As soon as I thought that, the light turned green, and the car slowly started moving forward. I unlocked my door and swung it open so hard. My instincts had me haul a%# back up the block toward my building. Thank God there was no such thing as child locks back then. My guy jumped out and yelled at me to get back into the car. The other guy started to drive the car backward and then stopped because cars started pulling up behind them. My guy never chased me, but I still ran for my life!!! Ya heard! FOR MY LIFE! I was so scared because I felt he had already held me hostage. What would he do with me if I stayed with him? I had trusted him but now was scared to death of him. I ran back up the hill and to my building. I got home and cried so hard in the bathroom. I was shaken and scared. All I kept thinking was that I left that little girl behind. I left her! She didn't even put up a fight...and never talked. I escaped, but she didn't. I was so scared for her. I wished I could've helped her more because she seemed more scared than I was. To this day, I think of her and what might've happened to her, and it's been nearly 30 years. In hindsight, I think we were victims of kidnapping for sex trafficking. Back then, I didn't know such a thing existed. I just know that I was scared and something wasn't right. I really think they were transporting us to another location for the same use. I only say that now, as I've grown and learned about it and look back at that situation. I realized this after I saw movies and thought "OMG!!! *That's exactly what happened to me.*"

I never heard from Hasaan again. He never contacted me, and I never tried to call him. I didn't realize it at the time but the more I kept thinking back to that last day, the more I remember he wasn't himself. He looked dirty and sloppy, his nose was running, and he was slurring. I wonder if he started using his own supply. The Ten Crack Commandments Rule #4: Never get high on your own supply. Yea, that's some straight Biggie lyrics. But that's all I can think of now when I reflect back.

I gave a chance to that guy who wasn't even my type just for him to treat me like that??? Almost had me involved in drug trafficking AND sex trafficking. It's crazy how he was this good guy to me, but things escalated and I had to escape. I say I "escaped," but we know it was by default how I got away. It was really nothing of my doing, unless they were novices at that type of thing and my big mouth scared them off from their original plan. By the grace of God looking out for me, they drove by my place for whatever reason. I don't know if they had planned to drop me off but changed their minds at the last minute. I mean, why else would they drive right past my building? I wonder if my big mouth (always asking questions) and my trying to fight him off were giving them second thoughts about keeping me. Maybe they said I was giving them too much hell so they would drop me off, but then changed their minds again? I really don't know. But Hasaan had never even seen me raise my voice, let alone be so feisty, until that day. So he definitely had a rude awakening. But thank God for His grace to keep me out of situations I wasn't even aware of. Thank God. He got me away safely.

A HARD BLUFF

For you are my hiding place; you protect me from trouble.

Psalm 32:7 (NLT)

Fast forward a few years to 1997. I was 20 years old. I was going back home, to my new apartment, in the middle of the night following fight night at a friend's house, when Tyson bit off Holyfield's ear. It was the first and last time I ever drove drunk. Why was I driving home drunk? Because a guy I was dating, Sammy, was supposed to be driving but was also drunk and passed out in the back seat. There I was, driving without a license. All I had was a permit, and I still needed to practice driving because I had just started learning to drive, or rather, he had just started teaching me. I was literally around the corner from my apartment and just happened to look in the rearview mirror to see flashing lights. I never heard the sirens, but wondered if I was so drunk I just didn't hear them. I pulled over and a cop walked up to the car. I rolled down my window. A bright flashlight shone in my face, then all around the car,

A Hard Bluff

and landed on Sammy in the back seat sprawled out. Officer: *"Why did you wait to pull over?"* Me: *"What?"* Officer: *"Why didn't you pull over back when you saw me turn the lights on? I've been following you for a couple of blocks now."* Me: *"Oh, I didn't realize you were trying to pull me over, officer. I just now saw the lights."* Officer: *"And you know you're driving down a one-way the wrong way?"* It was more of a statement than a question. I was new to the neighborhood so didn't know the area well. I looked around at the street sign at the end of the block. I couldn't tell which way it was facing. Nor did I see any parked cars to tell which way they were facing. Truthfully, they may have been there, but I was drunk and so shaken that I couldn't focus or think straight. All I was thinking was I was going to jail. *"No, I didn't know this was one-way."* Officer: *"Have you been drinking?"* Me: *"No, officer."* Officer: *"It smells like you were drinking."* I noticed a second officer near my car. Me: *"Well, I just had one drink."* I was just dying inside, knowing that he knew I was lying. Officer: *"Let me see your license and registration."* I thought, *"Oh, sh!t. I'm going to jail."* I bluffed. Me: *"Officer, I'm gonna be honest. I don't have my license on me. I left it at home because my boyfriend was supposed to be driving. But he was drinking and passed out, so I had to get us home. But if you let me go get it, I promise to bring it back to show it to you."* Officer: *"I can't just let you drive home. Where is home? Where do you live?"* Me: *"I live right around the corner."* Officer: *"Right around the corner?"* *"Yes, literally, on Chisholm Street."* He and the other officer turned around to talk and returned to me. He told me they would let me drive around to my place since I lived close by, and they would follow me and let me get my license to show them. *"OMG,"* I thought. *"I'm going to jail."*

The officers got back in their car and followed me around the block. I pulled to the front of my building and parked. Yes, there was parking right in front that night, or rather, early morning. Actually, my block wasn't bad on the parking back then. I think they were rebuilding abandoned buildings, so it was pretty much always an empty block. Officer: *"What floor do you live on?"* Me: *"Third. I'll just run up, get it, and bring it back down"* I said while thinking, *"OMG! I'm going to jail."* I thought I'd run up and stay upstairs, and they wouldn't be able to find what apartment I lived in. But then I remembered, *"Sh!t, Sammy is still knocked out in the car. I have to come back down."* I thought I'd return without it, saying I couldn't find it but show them my permit. Oh, my goodness. I was bluffing big time. At that moment, the officer said, *"Take your friend up with you and just bring your license back down."* So there I go, struggling with dead weight with my little ole drunk self, trying to pull Sammy out of the car and failing miserably. Talking to him, I pleaded with him to wake up and walk, pleading for him to help me a little. I wanted to cry. I started to get angry at him cuz I felt he left me out there fending for us both, and I was about to go to jail cuz his a%# got drunk and I was forced to drive us home. The anger plus the adrenaline of me going to jail gave me the strength to drag him out, hold him up against the car while he was falling over, and struggle to get him halfway over my shoulder. I was half dragging, half carrying him, and finally, after a few agonizing minutes, I started walking toward the building with him barely hanging on. We got to the outside building steps. Great. Now how was I going to get him to walk up the stairs? I couldn't carry him. I tried to half drag him up the steps. I don't remember how I made it halfway but between the sweat and tears, I was still holding Sammy up and looked at the commotion in the street. The cops got in their car and slammed the doors. I saw them drive off. They didn't say anything to me, just drove off. I would assume they didn't

A Hard Bluff

think I would go that far if I was lying to them or if I was just taking too long and wasting their time. Either way, Sammy felt like dead weight, and they could see the struggle was real.

Well, I got him up the steps and into the hallway lobby. How could I get him up another three flights? That was just the struggle to get him into the building. I just dropped him to the floor and started screaming at him. That jerked him awake with all the echo from the big empty lobby. I was so tired I sat down and bawled so hard, but I had so much relief. He had no clue what was going on. Still half drunk, he asked me why I was crying. I tried to tell him that because of him, I almost went to jail. He barely understood me. He stumbled up the stairs independently, and we crashed onto the bed. I told him the story the next day when we woke up. But I made it home. I escaped jail cuz I bluffed so hard. I knew how bad things could've gotten because the NYPD don't care about us in the "hood." Cops fractured my finger when I was a teen for no reason at all but for their own benefit and covered it up when I made a complaint. I had no good expectations of how they would treat us. So I understood it could've ended worse than a fracture or arrest. It's safe to say, letting me off easy was God's protection of angels sent down to cover me. I am grateful for His angels.

SURVIVING DEPRESSION

*Wait on the LORD: be of good courage, and
he shall strengthen thine heart:*

Psalm 27:14 (KJV)

By the time I was 22 years old in 1999, my drink of choice was screwdrivers (vodka and orange juice). With all the heavy drinking, I skipped weed and went straight to sniffing coke. At the same time, I was pregnant with my second child, living with baby daddy number two, and still engaging in both forms of substance abuse. One day I woke up drunk and high, and my lips were numb. I licked my lips. I felt nothing. So I licked them again. Nothing. I went to the bathroom to look in the mirror. Yup, my lips were still there, lol. Yes, waking up still half drunk out of my mind, for some reason I thought, *"Are my lips still on my face?"* Of course, they were, but one side of my lips was droopy. I put on chapstick to see if I could feel the stick gliding against my lips. Nothing. I went back to bed and woke up baby daddy, telling him something was wrong with my mouth.

Surviving Depression

We went to the clinic where I was getting my prenatal care. By that time, the whole right side of my face was droopy, and I couldn't close my right eye. I can't tell you how long we were there, but it was a while. The doctor didn't know what it was. I vaguely remember him bringing in another doctor, who didn't know my condition either. Doctors were going in and out of my room along with nurses and care team members. Everyone asked me questions. Finally, a nurse came in and told me my doctor was looking it up in his medical book and was going to put a call out to his colleague. Ok, yeah, that made me nervous. The doctor didn't even know what was going on with me? I didn't think I was dying, but all the commotion made me think it was more serious than I first thought. Finally, my doctor came back in with a diagnosis. Bell's Palsy. Huh? What? He explained it as a mini-stroke that affected the right side of my face. He also explained that it was caused by a lack of oxygen in my brain. He believed my baby was pulling too much of my oxygen to herself. The only way to treat it was to give me a steroid shot within 72 hours. I was within that window, but he said he couldn't give me the shot because I was pregnant and it could harm the baby. He also said it should go away on its own in 10 years. Ten years???!!! Once we received the diagnosis but learned there was no treatment, it was time to go home. If you think my engaging in substance abuse leading to Bell's Palsy was the end of it....just know that was the beginning of a tortuous pandora's box opening.

During my pregnancy, my Bell's Palsy progressed. My whole right side was affected. Not only were my lips droopy, I couldn't use a cup by itself or my drink would dribble down my face. I had to use a straw and physically close my lips with my fingers around it and sip. Then my right eye wouldn't close. Not even blink. It would just stay wide open. The doctor gave me drops

The Angels Are Watching

to moisten my eyes because staying open so long without blinking would dry them out. When I went to bed at night, I had to physically close my eyelid with my finger. Whenever I was outside, I wore sunglasses, even at night, looking crazy. One time my baby daddy and I were in the supermarket and people looked at me like, *"Why would she have them on inside the store?"* With all that going on, I went into a depression. I only realized this in hindsight because I wasn't aware of my feelings at the time. I just know I felt fat and ugly. I was thinking, *"Why would my boyfriend want to be with me looking like this?"* Whenever we went out together, people stared at me like a circus freak. All I did was cry at home and accuse him of cheating on me because I looked so hideous. And of course, he always reassured me that I was still beautiful and that he was not cheating on me. But that wasn't enough. I felt like he was just saying that to make me feel better.

Fast forward to after my daughter was born. I look back now and see all the stress I put her father through the first few months I stayed home with our newborn. There were many days when she cried that I cried along with her. Many days I felt like she was just there and that I had no connection with her as my daughter. I cared for her as a mother should for many days, feeding and bathing her. In between she sat in the baby swing all day until her father came home from work and held her. I felt no bond with her. Many days he would be driving on his way to work and I would call him on his cell phone and cry for him to come back home to get her because she was crying too much, and I didn't know how to make her stop. Mind you, I was on baby number two. Of course, I knew how to make her stop crying but for whatever reason, I didn't want to hold her and the swing wasn't doing its job. She wanted to be held and cuddled, but I couldn't pull myself to do it. So I would call him, pleading for him to come back. Sometimes he turned around before work and would just be late. Other times he was already at work and didn't return until his shift ended. One day, he came home from work with torn-out articles from magazines and was trying to give them to me. He told me they were articles about postpartum depression, and he thought I had it. I had never heard of the word or understood its meaning, but I knew the word depression was not me. So I didn't read the articles at that time. I didn't understand what it meant. I threw them away, knowing I wasn't depressed. I mean, why would I be depressed? Depression was a mental thing. I didn't have any mental issues. Or so I thought, right? Well, that was the end of him trying to help me. As time went on and before she turned one, life did change for me and her. I started to love her as I loved my firstborn son. I cared for her, cuddled with her, and finally bonded with her like nothing ever happened during the first few months of her life.

Looking back, I wonder who baby daddy was talking to about me at work. I am sure a woman gave him those articles. There is no way he thought of that on his own. Had he ever even heard of postpartum depression before then? I certainly hadn't. As I now know what it means, I did have it, unbeknownst to me. And I'm glad I didn't have it more severely because as I've read up on it since then, I've learned about mothers wanting to harm themselves and/or their baby and/or having bouts of suicidal thoughts. I never once thought of hurting her or myself. I just didn't want to touch her. Maybe I was depressed because I still felt ugly from the Bell's Palsy. I'm not sure, but I do thank God I got over the depression early enough to love on my baby girl while she was still an infant.

And about those 10 years after which the Bell's Palsy should've gone away...well, it's been about 25 years and it's still very noticeable to anyone who looks at me. I will say that by year 15, there had been a significant change in my face. My right side started not to droop as much. I could drink out of a regular cup without a straw, and I could blink and close my eyes without the help of my finger. But I still have the crooked lips when I talk or with my mouth closed, a crooked smile, and one-sided twitching to my eye and lips. I also have a deep crease on the right side of my face from the consistent tugging and the facial twitching. I try not to smile in my photos too much because you can see the significant lopsidedness of the right side of my face. One eye is closed more than the other, which is very noticeable in my pics. So I'll usually do a little smirk or no smile at all. Oftentimes, I look mean in my photos. People always tell me to smile, but they don't understand why I choose not to. The lopsidedness is too pronounced. So much for the 10 years of it going away on its own.

I look back and thank God He decided to give me the life-long effects of Bell's Palsy from my drug and alcohol use during my pregnancy instead of my daughter being impacted. I don't think I could live with myself if my daughter had life-long mental or physical issues because of the choices I made during her pregnancy, issues that could have been avoided. I rightfully own the consequences. I'm sure she was lacking oxygen herself with all the substance abuse, and that's why she had to pull extra from my supply to herself.

DOMESTIC VIOLENCE ARREST

In the day when I cried, thou answeredst me and strengthenedst me with strength in my soul.

Psalm 138:3 (KJV)

2001. By that time, I had moved to Charlotte, North Carolina, to live in a townhouse apartment on Dundeen Road to give my two young kids a better life than raising them in New York City. Or so I thought. I was living with Sammy... yup, back with him again. We definitely had a wild and toxic on-and-off relationship, but with mostly good times. I can not dispute it. But as we were young and growing together, there were also a lot of lessons we had to learn. Overall, he was a good guy who tried hard to keep us together as a family. Ultimately, it was just nothing but us growing up and growing apart.

Not to get too much into this story because it's more about my arrest than the details of why and how much of the situation occurred, but I need to give some context to explain how I was able to get into the military later. On one particular night, while my kids (ages three and almost two) were asleep in their shared room, another altercation started between me and Sammy in our bedroom on the upper floor. It started with him coming home drunk from the bar in the middle of the night and waking me up. He was mad because he said I was ignoring him, but I was sleeping. At some point between the punches being thrown by us, he got down deep and pulled up that throaty hock spit and patootie! Right square in my face. The next thing I remember was going to the closet, grabbing a wire hanger, retwisting it, pulling the hook upwards, putting it between my fingers, and starting to swing. Then I blacked out.

Next thing I knew, we were downstairs with the police banging at the door. I don't remember when we went down, and I don't remember which one of us answered the door. All I know is that two officers came in. They informed us they got a call from a neighbor who heard the screams. I was thinking, "*Nosy a%# neighbors who don't even speak to me, why????*" And who was screaming, him or me? Cuz I definitely blacked out and didn't remember any screaming. I only became alert when the banging on the door jerked me awake. We said we didn't want to file a report, but they took one look at us and said they had to. Then one said they had to take pictures of us. At that point, I still hadn't really looked at Sammy or myself, so I didn't know how bad the situation was. They started with taking pics of the both of us side by side. His bloody chest was cut up from the hanger, which I didn't remember doing. My face wasn't a pretty sight at that moment between the swelling and blood. Then they separated us to get our stories.

In my story, I said I was defending myself. His story was the same. They called their superior. One officer came back and said since they couldn't determine who was the defender and offender, they had to take us both in. I said I would go

Domestic Violence Arrest

with them so Sammy could stay home with the kids, so they wouldn't be taken into the system. Then he decided to man up and tell them he started the altercation and to take him in so I could stay with the kids. I thought, *"Now you want to do the right thing and tell the truth and get arrested for something you started in the first place??? Or your manly ego didn't like the way it looked that their mother was arrested while you stayed home with the kids, for something you started in the first place?"* Either way, we both said we started it so the other one could stay back with the kids. That didn't go well because then they couldn't determine who to let stay back. So yup, we both got arrested, and the kids were taken overnight to a foster family. We had 24 hours to get someone to pick them up or they would go into the child welfare system. Who could we get? There we were, alone in North Carolina with no family, trying to have a new beginning. Before we departed in separate cop cars, Sammy said he would reach out to his younger sister, Zakiya, in South Carolina, who happened to be away in college at the time. She originally lived in the Bronx, where we all were from but at that time, she was the closest family to us—a whole state away.

In my cell in an orange jumpsuit with a backed up, nasty a%# toilet and a backed-up sink that didn't work, I was on my face praying and crying out, *"God, please don't let them keep my kids! Please let Zakiya be able to get them in time."* That night, Sammy and I were both able to make one phone call before they put us in our cells. I prayed with his one call that he got word to her. I barely spoke to the other females in the common room the few days we were there. I remember sitting around them when they played card games but never joined when they asked me. All I kept thinking about was getting my kids back. And all I remember thinking was, *"Don't give away your food. Even if you're not hungry and someone asks for it,"* lol. I had no idea where that came from, but I ate what I wanted and threw away what I didn't want. No one ever asked me for my food anyway.

When we finally got our date in court for charges of "Assault or Simple Assault and Battery," we both pleaded not guilty. Based on our testimonies, the judge dismissed our case after he made us promise never to show up in his courtroom again for a domestic dispute or anything else. Well, there was more to it and why he let us go, but that was the gist of it. We were freed, and I could only think about getting my babies back from Zakiya, which was another thing.

I found out that she had just finished her finals and had taken off work to enjoy her spring break. And here we were, two older adults, interrupting her young and carefree life with our mess. We got the kids back from her only a few days into her break, but it was already ruined because she couldn't go away and enjoy the rest of what break she had left. We were only in lock-up for a short period of time, but any one day without my kids seemed like forever, especially knowing I had a 24-hour period to keep them out of the system. But I thank "Auntie" Zakiya to this day because if it weren't for her, this whole story would've turned out differently and not in a good way. When I cried out to God to keep my kids out of the system, He heard my cry and answered my prayer.

That orange jumpsuit was the real deal. And to this day, wire hangers are not allowed in my home. At all. Period.

After that ordeal, we moved back to the Bronx, New York. Back where we started. So much for a better life and new beginnings for our family.

7
NERVOUS BREAKDOWN

Don't be afraid, for I am with you. Don't be discouraged, for I am your God. I will strengthen you and help you. I will hold you up with my victorious right hand.

Isaiah 41:10 (NLT)

Fast forward to when I thought I was finally getting my life together in 2002. I returned to Charlotte, North Carolina, because I liked it there. I had lived there with Sammy until our arrest; then went back up to the Bronx; then down to Spartanburg, South Carolina, with family; and finally, back to Charlotte, North Carolina. I just didn't want to live in New York City . I was single again, caring for my two babies alone. I was in a different apartment on West Boulevard. Eventually, I enrolled in Chatty Hattie's School of Communications for TV/radio broadcast studies in Charlotte. The school did not provide or accept financial aid during that time, so I had to pay cash for tuition. Without child support or any financial help for my children, I had only one job to pay bills and my tuition. I just knew I could do it. I was going to prove to be this superwoman...or so I thought.

The struggle started getting real. I had to take an overnight job as the night auditor at the Clarion Hotel. Why overnight? Because it was the only hours that didn't interfere or overlap with me getting my kids to and from school or my broadcasting classes. I would pay different babysitters to keep them while I was in school and overnights while I worked, whoever was available. But there were more than a few nights I snuck them into work with me. I wasn't really sneaking them because I'm sure the airport shuttle driver, who doubled as overnight hotel security, was always watching my every move when I brought them in before my shift started. He was always early too. I guess he loved his job, but I was early cuz I had a different agenda. We were cool enough to speak and have some laughs throughout the shift, but he never mentioned me bringing my kids in, and neither did I. I would block out the rooms, as I was the only one running the front desk and booking rooms at night. I knew not to rent the room my kids slept in. I always put them on the lobby floor so that in case of emergencies, I could get to them quickly. I showed them how to press zero if they needed to ring mommy at the front desk, but I told them to make sure they didn't need mommy! I threatened them: No loud noises, no jumping on the beds, and leave the TV remote alone! They were to leave it on the channel I left it on for them to fall asleep to. I told them I would check on them periodically, which I did. They were usually asleep by my second check on them. If they needed ANYTHING, they could wait until I got back to them. Those were my rules for my babies. They adhered to them with no problems. In the morning following the nights they slept at the hotel while I worked, I took them juice and a donut or bagel from the continental breakfast because that's all the time they had for breakfast before getting back home and getting ready for school and daycare. I straightened up so the room looked like it wasn't used. How much of a mess could little kids make at bedtime, right? Yeah, that was my mindset back then. I know better now, lol.

I didn't have a car, so I was taking the city bus back and forth with the kids, to work, to my daughter's daycare because she wasn't in school yet, and sometimes to my school, although I got rides most times from friends. My oldest son's school bus picked him up and dropped him back at our apartment. But from the time I trekked us back home on the bus from my job in the mornings, I had to rush to get them ready for school and daycare, then started running all my errands. Back on the bus, with little to no sleep from the night before, day in and day out, just busy, busy, busy. Get the kids back from school and daycare, go to my school, back home, and back to work with the kids some nights.

And that's how I had my first nervous breakdown. One day, returning from running errands with shopping bags in my hands, I stepped off the bus at my stop and started walking home. I hit the little parking lot by the pizza place a few blocks up from my apartment, and my body gave out. I fell out in the middle of the street. Embarrassed, I half crawled with my bags and sat down on the side of the curb to the parking lot. I finally looked around to see if anyone saw me and bawled my eyes out. I was so weak, I had to stay sitting on the ground. I didn't understand what was happening and why my body acted like that. A few minutes later, a young but older than me Black man was driving by. He pulled over, got out of his car, and walked over to try and help me up. I was still sitting on the side of the street like a homeless person, still crying. I refused his help. I just needed to sit there. I was so done! Just tired. Mentally and physically tired. Exhausted and weak. Just flat-out burnt out! Tired, tired, tired of being a supermom. I just wanted to stay right where I was. He kept asking me if I was ok. Was I sure I didn't want his help? He said I could trust him and I didn't have to be scared because he was a teacher at such and such school (I forgot the name but I think it was an elementary school nearby that I had heard of, although not my son's school.) He assured me he could help me. I kept refusing. He eventually got back in his car hesitantly and drove off. I got myself together, got back up, and kept it moving, mentioning this to no one ever. The song "Can't Give Up Now" by Mary Mary repeatedly played in my head. Yes, I remember that. I went home and for the next few months, I had that song on repeat on my CD track. To this day, it's one of my favorites that got me through tough times. I definitely had it in rotation for the next few years and for the experiences shared in the next few stories.

    I had a second nervous breakdown years later when living in Columbus, Georgia, which was a little worse because the children were in the apartment with me when it happened. They were young, confused, scared, and didn't understand why mommy, out of nowhere for no reason, was banging the tennis racket against the wall, crying and screaming at the top of my lungs, *"I can't take this anymore. I'm tired of doing this all alone. I need help. Why do I keep going through this? Why me? I. Can't. Do. This. No More!"* Just burnt out all over again. I blacked out. After I came to, I collapsed on the floor. They sat around me, all three of them. By that time, I was a single mom with three kids. They had been standing there watching me with such fear. They surrounded me, asking questions: What's wrong? Can they help me? That made me feel worse and comforted at the same time. Worse because they were too young to witness me in despair like that. They didn't deserve to see their mom have such a meltdown. And comforting because they were right by me, trying to see what they could do to make me feel better. I don't remember what happened next, but I recall telling myself, "*OK, you cried it out. Now get your sh!t together. You can't let them see you like this. You're the mom. You're supposed to be taking care of them. Not the other way around.*" During my first breakdown in North Carolina, I didn't realize at the time what was happening. But that second time, I told myself I was having another breakdown. I was able to recognize it right away.

RAPE

... forgive one another if any of you has a grievance against someone. Forgive as the Lord forgave you.

Colossians 3:13 (NIV)

I met a girl. We became friends fast. I mean fast. Well, not friends, but acquaintances. She knew this guy and wanted me to keep the other guy company so she could hang out with her guy. She said they were ballers from out of town and had a lot of money. We were all in her empty apartment. They were all booed up, kissing, and sitting on the floor against the wall. She was sitting between his legs. There was nothing to sit on, so we were all sitting on the floor. The three of them were drinking and smoking weed, which the latter was never my thing. I was dry and sober for once, even though at the time I was still sniffing coke occasionally, but I didn't have any on me. I wasn't drinking that day either, which was very surprising because by then, I was an alcoholic. But with school and work, I didn't have the time to indulge like I was used to doing. I

Rape

remember feeling weirded out being there, and I didn't feel like drinking. At first, I was like, "*Who lives somewhere without any furniture?*" I kept looking around the empty apartment. Something didn't feel right, but I couldn't put my finger on it. I kind of remember feeling fake cuz I wasn't feeling ole boy there with me. I was nonchalant sitting by him, not wanting to be touched. He was trying and very handsy. I wasn't engaging in many conversations with him either. A movie was playing on a little TV sitting on the kitchen counter. I was acting like I was watching it. I wasn't interested in the guy or the movie. I just stayed because the girl asked me to stay to entertain the guy. He tried to get me interested in him. He offered to take me clothes shopping at the mall the next day, but I declined. He was surprised and he and my female acquaintance kept trying to persuade me to go shopping. I was disinterested in the guy and didn't want to give him mixed signals by spending his money. I don't use people like that.

The next day, he was out somewhere and called to ask me to go back with him to his hotel room to pick up his bag so he could see me one last time before he drove back home. I said he could stop by to see me. I didn't need to go with him. But he kept talking and said since he didn't get to take me shopping, he just wanted a little more than a few minutes to spend with me. He had the gift of gab and made me feel guilty. Please understand, I was young, cuz why would I feel guilty about not going shopping and not spending someone's money? Back then, I was such an honest person. I would've felt guilty if I did let him spend money on me knowing I didn't like him like that. So yeah, I didn't understand my mentality either. But he convinced me to ride with him to the hotel, then he'd drop me back home. When he came to get me, it was getting dark outside, so I had a neighbor from up the street come down to my apartment to watch my kids for a quick minute.

We got to the hotel, not the one I worked at, and he parked close to the front lobby. He asked me to go in with him. I said, "*No, I'll stay and wait in the car.*" He insisted on me sitting with him in the room for a few minutes while he packed his bag. It wouldn't take him long. Finally, I said ok and went inside with him. We walked through the front lobby, past the front desk. A young, tall, lanky, white guy was at the desk as we went down the hall and made a right. His room was on the lobby floor. We got inside. I sat on the bottom edge of the bed. He pulled out a small duffle bag and threw a few things in it. I don't remember if we were having a conversation or not, but I didn't feel threatened. When he finished packing, he started trying to kiss me. I kept pushing him off. That's when I could tell he had been drinking because I smelled it on his breath. Then we started fighting. I fought him off of me. He pulled my pants and panties down. I don't know how he got my pants down so easily. Maybe I had on leggings? I don't remember what I was wearing. But I do remember he had on sweatpants. I started screaming and crying while trying to fight him off of me again. He overpowered me, and the unthinkable happened. I tried pushing and fighting him. He just kept going and going. I went limp, exhausted from fighting. He finished fast, pulled up his pants, picked up his bag, and ran out the door. I laid there, still shocked.

When I decided to run after him a split second later to get his license plate number, I opened the door and saw him running down the opposite end from where we came in. I thought, "*What's down there? Where is he going?*" Just that quick, he turned the corner at the end of the hallway, and I returned to the front door the way we came in. I went outside to look for the Jeep, for the license number, but the Jeep was already gone!!! I went back to the front desk, still crying. I asked the receptionist what was down the opposite hallway and around the corner that I couldn't see. He said it was the back exit door. I asked him about the room number I was in. I didn't even know it because I blindly followed him in. Never thought to look at the door number. I asked what the guy's full name was because I only had a street name. He told me he couldn't give it to me for privacy purposes or whatever. I couldn't bring myself to tell him what the emergency was. I started acting hysterical and was upset that he wouldn't give me the guy's name. He asked whether I wanted to call the police, so maybe I told him I was raped in the hysteria. I don't remember what I said. But I told him I wasn't calling the police. I took my cell phone out of my pocketbook that was slung across both my shoulders this whole time, and the battery was dead (go figure). So I asked if I could use the desk phone to call someone to get me. I remember he kept giving me a sad look.

He let me use the desk phone. I didn't know who to call or who had a car to come to get me. I had a few options for friends, but I decided to call an African cab driver I barely knew. He was sometimes my cabbie ride to school, the grocery stores, and such. Why him? Because I didn't want to have to tell anyone else what happened. I was still crying and told him I was stranded, asked him to come to get me, and said I didn't have money to pay him. I waited on the lobby couch until he came. He walked in to get me. When we got in the car, the questions started. He asked how I got stranded there. Why was I there? I started crying all over again and blurted out to him that some guy brought me there and raped me. Of course, he asked me questions about the guy. I had no answers cuz I had just met the guy the day before. Didn't have a name, an address, or even what state he lived in. He was a dope boy on a drug transport run, according to the girl I barely knew. Ohhh, why did I say anything? The cabbie got mad and became nasty and mean with his heavy accent, saying what did I think would happen with me going into a hotel room??? How could I be so stupid? I should've known he wanted sex! Yada, yada, yada. On and on his rant went. He said if I wanted to report the guy, what would the cops think of me saying I went into the hotel at night with a guy when I didn't even know his real name? I started thinking it was all my fault that the rape happened. I should've known better than to go in. I should've just stuck to my first thought and waited in the car, or better yet, stayed home. I felt guilty and ashamed that I was so stupid to let this happen to me.

I got home and cried and cried and cried. I was mad at myself. I put up a fight. I did. A really big fight. How could I lose? To him? I've fought off bigger people than him when I was younger. All the fighting I used to do. Fighting guys and girls. Was it the awkward position I was in on the bed? Was I so fatigued and weak from everyday life? Was it all the coke and alcohol in my system that finally caught up to me that had me weak? Wasn't the adrenaline pumping throughout my body supposed to make me super strong? All the excuses, but I still blamed myself. I lost the battle. My mind gave in to blame, guilt, and shame. I cried myself to sleep.

After that incident, I never heard from the girl and I never called her again. I wonder if she knew about what happened to me. I just couldn't bring myself to be around her again. I didn't blame her, but if she heard anything, I didn't want to be answering her questions. It was many years before I stopped blaming myself, about 20 years later.

The back story is about how I met the younger girl and why I barely knew her. We met through her older sister. Her sister and I were about the same age and met at a warehouse when I was working a job I got through a temp agency. I worked the mornings cuz I needed to work two jobs to help pay the tuition or I would've gotten dropped from school. My hotel job barely paid my bills and the necessities for the kids and me. On the last day of that temporary assignment, the younger sister came to pick up the girl I worked with. We met and hit it off. She kept saying I was pretty and such. I thought she might've liked me sexually at the time, but in hindsight, she wanted to use me as a pawn to keep the one guy busy. But where were her real friends? She could've asked them. Good question, but that doesn't help me to know the answer now.

After we met, she came to my house only once. We had drinks, listened to music, just hanging out in my living room while my kids were playing in their room. That day she told me her guy friend would be coming from out of town to hang out with her and for me to come along to meet his friend, also from out of town. I was down for the free drinks. So that was the first time we hung out, at my place. The second time, a couple of days later, they picked me up in the jeep, and we went to the girl's apartment that had no furniture. So our friendship was short-lived. This happened in 2002, not long after my nervous breakdown in the street. Besides the cab driver who picked me up and maybe the front desk clerk I may have told in my hysteria, I never told anyone else this story until 2021. Then it was only because another female told me about her rape encounter first and how she felt stupid (her word) and naïve to let it happen by someone she actually knew. Then I felt comfortable enough to tell her and not feel ashamed because I felt dumb that I was so naïve too. I knew she wouldn't judge me, as I didn't judge her.

As for forgiveness, I never heard from him again so I was never given an apology. Forgiveness is not easy, especially when someone schemed to harm you. But now, with my healing process, I've chosen to forgive him. Not for him, but for me to be able to accept and move past the anger, hatred, bitterness, misery, and resentment toward him, the incident, and myself. Not only did I forgive him in my heart, I forgave myself for my own guilt and shame and for judging myself so harshly for something I had no control over. At first, I spoke of forgiveness but didn't feel it. I had to ask God to let me "feel" it in my heart and not just say I forgave out my mouth. Over time, as always, He answered my prayer. It's because of God that I am at peace with it now. I can talk about it after all these years, and God can use my experience to help others. I wonder what has become of that guy today. Not that I really care to know, but does he still think about that day or have remorse for what he did? What would make him do that to someone? Honestly, I feel that wasn't his first time, the way he was so smooth and conniving and had an escape plan. But I am free mentally and I have peace now. It's not for me to judge him. I leave the judgment to God. Hopefully, he repents of his sins to God before the end of his earthly life and before the rapture.

CRACK ADDICTION 9

Deliver me in thy righteousness, and cause me to escape: incline thine ear unto me, and save me.

Psalm 71:2 (KJV)

How I got hooked on crack and delivered was a roller coaster ride. I will save you the gruesome, intimate details of being in my crack addiction. I have many stories of unimaginable things that I have been involved in or witnessed that would rock you to the core. But I will give you the "Mary Poppins" version, just the surface of the story. I will spare you all the extreme stories about what you would see in a crack house or in one's crack addiction, as this is only a generalization of my addiction.

For a while before the rape, I had slowed down with sniffing coke and drinking so much because I was in school, working two jobs, and busy throughout the day with my kids. Being busy kept me occupied for a while, with not much free time to enjoy anything I deemed "fun." So the times I dipped and dabbled were very few and far between, much less than indulging every day as I once had. I was sniffing about four to five years before I got hooked on crack. Writing this book was therapeutic and now I see the sequence of events throughout my life and how I started harder drugs after the rape. I never put the two together back then. I had put it to the back of my mind all these years and never realized it until now.

    I was still living as a single mom in the apartment complex on West Boulevard in Charlotte, North Carolina. I was back down to one job cuz the temp position was over. A neighbor who lived in my same building was heavy into crack, but she was a functioning drug addict and was very good to me and my kids. If you didn't know her, you wouldn't know she had an addiction. She even ran around in the back of our apartment complex to help teach my oldest son how to ride his bike without training wheels. She really looked out for us because she had lived there many years before I and the kids arrived. She knew everybody in the neighborhood and had them look out for us as well. She pretty much ran a party house with all types of drugs, alcohol, and music running through her apartment every night. As a functioning addict, she was able to work during the day, be up all night partying, and back to work the next day. Everybody always had a good time there.

    Every once in a while, when I had a night off and the kids were in bed, I'd go downstairs, have a seat, sniff my coke, drink my beer for a little, and head back up to my apartment. It was just so I would be around company and not alone in my place. Everyone had their own drug of choice (DOC), but theirs was mostly weed, ecstasy, and crack. I was the only one sniffing every time I was there. She used to ALWAYS tell me, *"Don't ever try crack! Not even once."* She said I had too much going for me and my kids. But I thought, *"Didn't they all? Why was I any*

Crack Addiction

different than her or the rest of the people there?" But she always checked anyone she thought was trying to give it to me and made sure to keep them away from me as much as possible.

One night at her apartment, I ran out of coke before I was ready to go back up to my place. I called my dealer and he was out. All he had on him was weed. Everyone there had different dealers but only mine had the coke supply. With him out and no one else's dealer able to get me any cuz yes, I asked around, my question was, *"Do I go back upstairs or stay and smoke the weed?"* Well, I didn't want to leave, as I was having a good time and weed made me sleepy. I didn't want to be there being the party pooper, falling asleep when everyone else was live. So I asked what else he had for me. Ecstasy, if I waited for him to cop it from someone else. *"Damn, that's it? They don't have coke either? Ok, I'll take that."* Later, I went to meet up with him outside. I took another female I had gotten to know from being in my neighbor's apartment from time to time. My dealer told me to take half the pill and the other half later since it was my first time. Yea, he knew it was my first time, cuz I was asking him all the questions about it, lol. I had heard about it but never tried it. Looking back, what kind of help was that when he was selling it to me anyway, lol? But a drug dealer is a drug dealer, right? *"Ok, I'll cut it in half,"* I said. I paid him and we went back into the apartment.

We got back inside and my neighbor asked, *"What's up?"* Just her being casual. I said, *"I'm good now."* She asked what I got cuz she knew my dealer didn't have any more coke. She just wanted to make sure I didn't get crack cuz the other girl was with me and that was her DOC. Ole girl with me was like, *"Yea, she just copped some X, she good now."* So now, neighbor girl is concerned cuz why would I buy that? That's not my DOC. I said, *"He didn't have any coke and I wanted something."* So she

47

The Angels Are Watching

went back and forth with me about me taking something new. I let her know I was only taking half and would be ok. That wasn't good enough for her. We were getting loud in front of everybody so she chilled and gave in. We walked to the kitchen so she could cut the pill in half for me. I took it out of the baggie and handed it to her to cut like the dumb a%# I was, and she ran and flushed it with me chasing behind her, watching it go down the toilet. Money wasted. Mad, but not mad enough. Why not mad enough? Because instead of me cursing her out and going back to my apartment, I sat my mad a%# right down on her couch and popped open a new beer. Wheels spinning..."*What can I do now?*" I didn't want to go back upstairs to my boring apartment. I just needed to get some coke from somewhere and stay and chill with everybody around. Somebody out there in the streets had to have some.

Sitting there thinking, the guy at the other end of the couch moved closer to me. Someone I had never seen at ole girl's apartment before. He asked me, "*What's up?*" I told him I ran out of coke. He said he'd share his rock with me. What do I do now? I tell him I can't cuz my neighbor, aka mother hen, is somewhere around watching me. Plus, I didn't know how to smoke it being that I never tried it. His solution? He would give me a shotgun (smoke it and blow it into my mouth) and I would just inhale. He said it would give me less of an effect than smoking it straight up since it's my first time. How could I go wrong with that? Either I try it, stay longer and hang out, or I go back upstairs to sleeping kids, right? Whelp, based off this chapter title, you know what I decided. Making sure "mother neighbor" was out of sight, that was how and when I had my first semi-hit. Then another. And eventually, another.

Sometime during the night, I must've been acting really weird. All I remember was standing up in front of mother neighbor with her grilling me and asking me questions I couldn't answer. I was stuck. I was hearing her but couldn't get the words out to answer. I was feeling so high—at that time the word "nice" came to my mind. It sounded better. She knew something was up. The guy decided to say something. Oh great! Here we go! He told her he was giving me shotguns. That's all I remember before I heard the noise. My high mind was trying to figure out what was that awful sound. She was wailing like a wounded animal. When he told her, she fell to her knees bawling and screaming, *"Nnnnoooooo!!!"* with true, sincere anguish in her voice. I'll never forget that cry. She sounded like she really cared and was hurt by my actions, but mainly sounded like a wounded animal. She got up off her knees and started cursing me out, with tears running down her face. But this time was different. It was like never before. She told me over and over that I should've listened to her. That I should've never tried it. I got that she really did care about me, but it was hard to take someone that serious when the pot was calling the kettle black. And what did she think was gonna happen eventually with me being there so much? Anyway, I just stood there and let her yell at me. But in my mind I was thinking, *"It's not that bad. I'm feeling nice, but I'm not gonna get addicted. Plus, I'm still functioning. How bad could it be? Right?"* Well, I was wrong.

All these years, I thought I got hooked because I ran out of my first DOC, coke, which may have been the case. But let's be real: Who wants to be left in their own thoughts in an apartment alone after a rape? Not exactly alone, I had small kids. But what kind of consolation could they give me at their age? All I did was keep it to myself and blame myself whenever I was left alone to my own thoughts. I didn't understand my thought process. I didn't put the two together, the timeline of events or that the rape triggered my need to mask my trauma more and more with drugs. I realize now that I didn't want to be alone in my apartment. The nights I had to work at the hotel kept my mind occupied. But what about the nights I was off? I couldn't shake the feeling that I should've known better. I should have done things differently. If only I didn't go with him...No excuses are needed because I did what I wanted to do to get high, but I now see the sequence of events that led me down that road. I continued to use at any cost to stay around people so I wouldn't be left alone.

So I continued to see the guy after that night. More like, I continued to do shotguns with him at her place from time to time. We exchanged numbers and then one day, while the kids were in school, he took me over to his place to "watch a movie." I expected him to push up on me, but we never had sex. At that point, I still hadn't had any sex since my rape. Ironically, I was interested enough to go by his place alone. Maybe, subconsciously, I knew he would offer me a hit cuz I definitely wasn't interested in him or to watch a movie. Whelp! He indeed offered me my first real hit right there on his living room couch. He showed me how to hold the pipe and how to inhale. He lit it for me, I inhaled, and the next thing I remember was being on the floor in his bathroom, holding onto the toilet seat while throwing up. My eyes were tearing down my face. I kept gagging and thinking it was the most awful feeling I had ever felt. He kept calling out to me from the living room, asking if I was ok. I assured him I was, but I was still nauseous. It didn't matter that I had thrown up, the feeling was still there. I cleaned myself up and walked back to him. The initial sickening feeling started to subside, and I started to feel like I was floating. The high kicked in and smoothed out. Now, that feeling I could get used to. And that was the beginning of my crack addiction.

Crack Addiction

For a while after that, I would kick it with him from time to time. He would always have the supply, the paraphernalia, and the beer. Can't forget the good ole beer. As time went on, I lost touch with him. I don't remember much, but I think it had to do with me starting to hang out at my own place and smoking. I had my mother neighbor and her "friends" show me how to build my own homemade pipes from a pen with copper brillo and such. So I was doing my own grown woman things. I started buying my own supply, since I didn't have ole boy around me anymore. One thing I quickly learned, no one shares their rocks like my dude did with me. It was every man for themselves. So with that, I had no more freebees and just one small rock was so expensive. Yea, it was much more expensive than when I was buying coke, and it lasted you just a few pulls. So even though my house became the smokehouse, nobody shared with me. I was on my own.

Time went on and I realized my apartment had become the new party house because mother neighbor had moved into her boyfriend's house. Like I said before, she was a functioning addict. She always kept a job and a man. So now everybody in the neighborhood was smoking, drinking, and playing loud music at my place. Yup, and with my small kids around. My mind was so jaded most of the time, I didn't understand how detrimental it was to my kids back then. I would keep them in their rooms when they came home from school, but I realize now that wasn't enough. I know now they grew up witnessing a lot more than I thought.

I was still working at the hotel overnight and still going to broadcasting school when luckily for me (no, not really lucky) my siblings and I inherited money from my deceased dad. Every week I would call my mom, who I had purposely put in charge of my money so I wouldn't spend it, to ask her for my money. After the first few months, she asked me why I needed a hundred dollars every week. (A hundred dollars went a longer way back then.) I lied and told her the money I was making from my job was just enough to cover my tuition and some bills. I needed more money to help with the babysitters I had for my kids, you know, since I was a single parent and wasn't getting any child support and such. That was my excuse. And that lie held me for a little bit. In between work, school, and the kids, I was able to spread the money from her and my paychecks evenly throughout the week for the drugs in my downtime. The more I became addicted, the more during the week I would call my mom and ask for money before the week was out. Let's pause here cuz as this was going on, I had two more things happening at the same time.

The first was about my job. At my hotel job, I had begun to get sloppy and had lost so much weight. People were starting to question me about my uniform being so baggy. They knew I took pride in myself and the way I dressed, even if it was just a uniform. Well, that's when the shame started. I knew they knew. Even though I thought I was a functioning addict, I knew they saw differently. But that didn't stop me. Like I said, I was getting sloppy, and not just physically. One day, my boss asked me to work a day shift cuz remember, I was still working nights. I said, *"Of course."* Well, that's the day I happened to be irritated, probably cuz I needed another hit from being up all night smoking. So, I was answering phones to book rooms. I spoke to this one guest and went back and forth about what accommodations she couldn't have. For whatever reason, I wasn't giving her any discounts. She didn't have the proper reasons or privileges to get any, and I wasn't trying to be generous just because. I was being nasty to her and slammed the phone down while she was still talking. I

Crack Addiction

remember thinking, "*Wow! This is not like me to be arguing with a guest.*" That was definitely out of character for me. I would curse someone out in the street, but I took my jobs very seriously.

Next thing I knew, my general manager pulled me away. We went outside to sit on the bench and talk. He told me a secret shopper called and I was very rude to her. Yes, that's when everywhere had those secret shoppers. But did they really set me up at the job? Did they have someone on the inside they knew to test me because of my behavior? Or was that really a secret shopper? I would never really know because again, that was the time when the secret shoppers were a big deal. I even thought to get myself a part-time job doing that at one point. At any rate, he said I failed my company miserably. He asked me what was going on because, as I already knew, I was one of his best employees. He spoke so highly of me, and things weren't looking too good with my behavior. I just broke down and said I had an addiction problem I was fighting. But instead of a drug addiction, I told him it was an alcohol addiction. He told me to call and have my mom come down to help me and my kids until I get better. That was his first solution. I told him I could not do that. My mom had her own life and I wouldn't dare ask her to take time off from her job to come down to me. So then he suggested I take time off from work and school and go into rehab. He promised he would hold my job for me when I came back out. I know he knew it was a drug addiction, but he never mentioned it and neither did I. I told him I would do exactly that and thanked him for his care and concern. That was my last day there because my addiction only got worse, and I never went back.

Without a job, I was asking my mom for even more money during the week instead of on a weekly basis cuz let's be real, I had barely been spending my money to pay for the bills anyway. With my paycheck money and my inheritance my mom was sending me, I was good to go with keeping a stash of drugs and not running out every week. But as time was winding down on the paychecks, I was asking her for money more times during the week to try to hold onto what I had left. And that's how she found out. She questioned why I needed so much money all the time. The lies kept flowing until the pressure and questions kept coming, and I finally broke down and told her. All I remembered was dead silence for a few seconds, that seemed like forever, and me saying *"Bye"* and I hung up. I knew her answer would be no so why stay on the phone? That was the last time I remember hearing from her for a while. And the money—my inheritance—stopped coming from her. Without working, I had more time to be home to smoke with the last few checks I had left. I found out later from my cousin that when my mom had gotten off the call, she was sobbing so hard and called her sister, my aunt, and couldn't be consoled. And that's how the rest of my family found out.

Like I said, there was another thing going on at this time, and that was with my children. Then there was Ms. Bo. Good ole Ms. Bonita Goode was a woman who worked at my kids' daycare. My daughter was there all day, and my son attended the after-school care there. One day, out of nowhere, I looked up and noticed this woman was dropping them home to me when the daycare let out. I never really remembered when it all started or why. Was I always late to pick them up? I don't remember but I know I was always so high. I just looked around one day and there she was. She would bring them home to me safe and talk with me briefly. I assume now that she was casing their environment during her drop offs. One Friday, she asked to take them to her family's cookout the next day on Saturday and I agreed. When she brought them home that Saturday night, she asked me if I had been feeding them. Me: *"Of course, yes."* Her: *"Then why they ate two and three plates like they haven't eaten in days??!!! They were hungry!!!"* Oooh, she was big mad at me. On and on she went. She went so hard for them. She told me I thought I could fool her, but she's had family members on drugs and she knew I was on drugs. I was not fooling her, and I was not taking care of them or feeding them. She said I should be ashamed for choosing drugs over them. And she never let up.

At first, I denied everything. But after she said the part about how I couldn't fool her, I just sat down at the kitchen table and kept my mouth shut with my head hung. Standing over me, she ripped into me and told me she would be coming to get them to stay with her every weekend from there on out. She said she would keep them during the week if she could, but she worked two jobs and didn't have the time to keep them. That was how she began taking care of my kids. When she left, I cried so hard because I didn't realize I hadn't really been feeding them at home. They had pop tarts, cereal and stuff, but not cooked meals anymore. Because someone finally confronted me about my addiction, I couldn't deny it anymore. I felt so ashamed. And that's how Ms. Bo came into our lives. Never no real introduction to each other. I just looked up and there she was at the right time. God sent us an angel. To this day, we still call her and go visit her when we pass through North Carolina. If it wasn't for her, the situation would have definitely been worse. God sent this loving and caring woman to step in when we needed her the most, especially my children. She kept them loved and together. She would get them faithfully, every Friday through Sunday, until the day they were taken from me and sent back to my mom in New York.

So now, back to the original story...I no longer worked. I saw I was neglecting my kids. It was time to make a change. I had always made sure I took care of my kids, so now wouldn't be any different. So, I made a plan. First, I talked to my school to tell them I was going into rehab for my drinking. They agreed to let me take off 30 days and assured me that they would modify my schoolwork so that when I came out, I would be able to catch up and graduate on time with everyone else.

Then I called baby daddy number two in New York. I asked him to come down for the 30 days I would be in rehab to care for the kids and keep them in their school and daycare until I came back home. He agreed and came down. I already had my little duffle bag packed. I was all set. I was gonna get clean and get my life back on track. This was going to be too easy, or so I thought.

FRAGO! FRAGO!! FRAGO!!!

He came and the next thing I knew, he was on the phone with my mom, telling her the situation was worse than I made him believe. He said that everything was a mess at my place. Maybe that wasn't the nicest words he used. But in other words, the apartment was dirty and the kids were dirty and only eating cereal because that's all I had in the house. At that point, I couldn't recall the last time I had gone grocery shopping or even bathed them. I didn't see everything as bad as he did because I was always under the influence. I do know for sure that I hadn't had any appetite to eat while I was smoking, and I was wasting away in my clothes, so yes, perhaps there wasn't any real food of substance in my apartment. I believe now, looking back, that before he came to help me, he may have thought I was in the beginning of my addiction and was trying to catch it before it got worse. But in fact, it was worse and probably very much right before my rock bottom because my money was running out. So he was here, on the phone, and my mom was telling him to bring the kids up to her in New York.

How did this all unfold? I told him he was not taking my kids from me. All those years, I struggled by myself with no one's help. Now they wanted to "help" by taking my kids? I told him, *"NO! No way!"* We argued. He tried to get them ready so they could leave with him. We argued some more. I pulled a big butcher knife out of the kitchen drawer and threatened to stab him. I said he wasn't taking them anywhere. He called the police. A Black female and white male officer came, listened to his story, and had him call my mom and put her on speaker phone. The female officer actually did the talking with my mom. They spoke with her and were assured she would take good care of them. My mom told me that once I cleaned myself up and showed her I could stay clean, she would give me my kids back. The end result? The female officer convinced me to let baby daddy take them back up to my mom in the Bronx. She actually said my mom and baby daddy really seemed to be trying to help me. *"You say, you want to get clean. Let her keep them until you get out of rehab,"* she said. Then she told me if I didn't let them go, knowing my situation, they would have to come back and take my kids and place them with Child Protective Services because their environment was unhealthy. So I forcefully and reluctantly packed their bags and let them go up to my mom.

My addiction didn't numb me enough because I literally cried all day for days. I carried their pictures around the apartment while crying. Every time my dealer came, I would show him their pics and said one day I would get them back. Funny story: He acted like he cared, but of course he would say whatever to make a sale. Logically, how would I get them back when all I continued to do was smoke all day every day?

I didn't have a care in the world anymore. I lost what little motivation I once had to go into rehab. It was all gone. No desire whatsoever. The plan was for baby daddy to come down to help keep them at my apartment while I went away to help myself. But the end result was they were taken from me, to be cared for nonetheless, but in my mind I asked for help and my kids were stolen from me. Yes, that's the word I kept using. Baby daddy and my mom "stole" my kids from me. I told anybody and everybody who heard my story that they were stolen from me. Of course, I know now it was done out of love. At the time, I was left alone and depressed. My kids were truly my world.

Around that time, Ms. Bo had been picking them up every weekend. I had stopped everyone from coming over to my apartment, "the crack house" at night while the kids were in bed, cuz I realized people were stealing things to sell to get more drugs. I put a stop to it but a lot of things were already gone by the time I realized it. Even some of my kids' stuff was stolen out of their bedroom they shared. So everyone got kicked out and had to find another place to do their drugs. With my kids gone, no one around to smoke or hang out with, it was just me and the empty apartment and the drugs. Alone. Me, crying to God every day to help me stop. But I just could not.

Remember my homegirls Jaime and Tasha? From the time my mom had found out about my addiction earlier, so did they. I would always call Tasha, still up in New York, and cry to her and ask her to help me stop. She would stay up all night with me on the phone, praying over me and reading scriptures out of her Bible until I fell asleep on the phone, like a mother reading a bedtime story to her child. I don't remember how many nights she stayed up with me because I was always high and time wasn't a thing I kept track of, but she never complained and never not answered her phone when I called. I'm sure many mornings she went to work tired. But again, she never complained to me. So when the kids were taken from me, she went even harder for me, all those nights on the phone. And yet, I still used.

Now's the time to tell you about Stan, my good friend in Charlotte, North Carolina. Why a good friend? Because he always looked out for me and my kids, from day one when we moved there, but stayed in the background. Up until that point, he just went with my flow, not trying to step on my toes, not trying to piss me off. But when the kids got taken from me, he had enough of my sh!t! We lived in the same neighborhood, him being there most his life and me being the newbie on the block. When I didn't want to take the bus and we needed a ride somewhere, like the supermarket, work, school, etc., he had us. There were times he tried to "clean house" in my apartment when everyone was there smoking, but I stopped him. But whatever I needed help with, he was there for me and the kids. He saw me go from a clean girl to deteriorated on drugs. He tried to step in to help, but he could only do so much. I believe he wanted to stay around to make sure we were safe. When he would come around and people were in my apartment, they would straighten up if they were acting a fool or even leave cuz he was there. They knew how to behave when he was around. He was pretty much known in the neighborhood as the guy not to be f^&ed with. I really think he stayed around for the safety of me and the kids, to keep things in order as much as he could. When things got bad, he convinced me to give him a copy of my key so he could check on us.

But again... he had enough of my mess! The kids being taken was the last straw because he knew how much I loved and used to take care of them when I first arrived there. My two prides of joy. Well, he was done playing nice with me.

One day, he let himself in with his key and I was sitting on the edge of my bed smoking. He said, *"You was supposed to be going to rehab. This all happened so you can get clean."* I said, *"I'm not ready yet. I'll go tomorrow."* He said, *"You said that yesterday."* Did I? I didn't remember. I had been smoking my last few checks and didn't have the kids, so I didn't have a care in the world, except for the nights I would call Tasha crying. Whelp! That was all he wrote. He looked down at my bag near my bed. He said, *"That's your packed bag?"* I said, *"Yup."* He picked it up and snatched my pipe straight from my lips and walked out my door with it in his hands. And what did I do? Follow right behind him screaming, cursing him out, telling him to give me back my pipe. This man had the audacity to go to the edge of the woods, behind my apartment complex, and toss my pipe so far! I just stood there speechless for I don't know how long. I was debating going to look for it, but I knew I would not find it. There I was standing, staring into the woods, looking stupid. Next thing I knew, he literally grabbed me up off the ground and struggled to put me in his car. We were fighting the whole time cuz I told him I was not going to rehab and he told me I was. Well, he got me and my bag in the car and locked the doors. Yes, I could've gotten out. But truthfully, my mind was so clouded at the time. All I thought about was my rock that he wasted. Gone. I didn't think to unlock the door and run back to my apartment. That would've been the easiest and most logical thing to do. But what did I do? Just sat there, screamed, cried, and cursed him out the whole way while banging and kicking the door and window, trying to break them. Why? I don't know, maybe to show him I wasn't going down without a fight? He was quiet the whole way. Never looked at me. Never said a word. And no, I never broke the window. When we arrived at the facility, I walked in quietly with him. I knew that was it. I had to go. But I was not happy. We got to the front desk and he gave my info and filled out the paperwork, as much as he knew. They told me they needed my signature to sign myself in. I said, *"Oh, so if I don't sign myself in, I don't have to stay?"* That was correct. So for a split second, I almost turned around to leave. But I looked at Stan and saw he really was trying to help me, so I just signed the papers. Ughhhh. Then they took my cell phone. They said I could only use their free phone. Damn, I didn't remember anybody's numbers because I would be so high, so I guessed I wouldn't be calling anybody anytime soon. I thought, *"Ok, let's do these 30 days so I can get my phone back and go back home."*

My one and only phone call on their free public wall phone was to Regina. I don't know how I remembered her phone number of all people. Being hazy in the brain, I can assure you, I didn't remember many numbers, especially ones I hadn't called in a while. But after a couple of days of being there, I called her. She was another female I met in North Carolina at a bus stop going to a course at Central Piedmont Community College to get our Medical Reimbursement Certificate before I went into broadcasting school. Meeting at the bus stop and realizing we were going to the same school and class, we were hyped! If I remember correctly, when I first got down to North Carolina and was on welfare, they helped me get into the program. Regina and I became the best of friends quick. We both were single parents, no fathers or child support involved. I had two kids. She had three. They were all around the same age. We were both new to Charlotte from out of state, so we literally knew no one else. I had met her before even meeting "mother neighbor" or Stan. Regina never knew about my addictions. Seeing her during the daytime and hanging out downstairs at mother neighbor's apartment at nights, Regina never suspected a thing. I kept the two separate. We lived a couple of blocks from each other within walking distance and neither one of us had a car. We became good friends, taking turns cooking Sunday dinners at each other's places for our kids and our sisterhood friendship. But as much of a friendship we had, I never mentioned the drugs or rape to her. We always kept in touch until my crack addiction took over. I slowly weaned myself away from her.

Regina. That one call. We talked and she was asking me questions. Where had I been?, etc. She had been calling me and trying to find me because I never answered my phone or door anymore at that point. She thought I moved back to New York because she could never get in touch with me. Well, when she found out I was in rehab, she screamed at me out of love. She asked why I didn't ask her for help and realized why I had been avoiding her. She thought she did something wrong to me and couldn't figure out why I stopped talking to her. After the anguish she displayed when I told her the kids were "stolen" from me, she finally calmed down and thanked me for reaching out to her so she could be around to help me now. We had always encouraged each other as single parents and friends, and she truly was the encouraging friend I needed at that time. Just like Tasha, but Regina was closer in location. They both let me know they had my back and everything would be ok because they were there to help me through. Since then, we've never lost touch, over 20 years later, as she kept her word. To this day, Regina checks on me and the kids and now, well now, it goes both ways.

She was my one phone call of peace. Not Tasha, not Stan because I was still mad at him for taking me there, and not my mom because I was mad she stole my kids. I always wondered why her? Why Regina? Only God knew. After the reassurances of my good friend, I did the rest of my bid at the rehab. I only called her that one time and never called anyone else except on the last day, when it was time to leave and I called for a ride home.

Early on while doing my time, I remember one night in bed going through physical withdrawals and shaking, more like spasms, tossing and turning all night. I remember making little noises that kept slipping out of my mouth that I kept trying to control. I did not get any sleep. The next morning, I asked my white female roommate if I had kept her up. Was I making too much noise overnight with my tweaking sounds and all the jerky spasm movements? She told me she had slept well, hadn't even heard me the whole night. I thought, *"Wow, good for her. I hope I can sleep like that again soon."* Truthfully, I only remember that one night of going through major withdrawals. I would've thought, hearing from all the other patients in the group sessions, that I would have experienced it more.

As I was nearing the end of my stay, a Black male patient arrived at the facility. I had never seen him before but truth be told, I paid everyone no mind. I barely spoke to the other patients. I was a loner in there. I just wanted to finish my program and go home. I did what I was told, going through the motions. I didn't feel like it was helping, but of course I would not tell my counselors that. They heard from my mouth exactly what they wanted to hear. Nothing more, nothing less. So, I honestly didn't notice who had been there all along. If you weren't in any of my group therapies I had to attend day in and day out, then I didn't even notice you. But there he was. One day on a break in the day room, he sat next to me at the table. Never introduced himself or anything, just started telling me he wanted to hang out with me when we both got out and he could get me some free crack so we could kick it. Wow! This man had been watching me. He must've been in one of my group therapies, where we all had to talk, and I hadn't noticed because he knew my drug of choice and everything.

    Honestly, it took me a second to respond cuz truthfully, that whole time in the facility, all I could think about was getting another hit. Nothing like that first hit after not smoking for a while. It was on my mind heavy. I was nearing the end of my program and now some free crack when I got out! I ain't even gonna lie, I did hesitate for a quick second because I had no money left. Wasn't even sure how I would get that first hit when I got out. I was thinking about whatever else I had left in my apartment to sell since everybody already stole so much from me. But then I really looked at him in his face. I was so disgusted. I'm thinking, *"How is he gonna just help me relapse? Aren't we here to get ourselves better? How dare he be my downfall. I can be my own downfall."* It just didn't make sense. Next, I was thinking, *"Yea, he just wants sex. He must think I'm cute or something because I already know the game."* I had been deep in the game by then, been around and seen and heard a lot. A whole lot I didn't share in this book. So really looking at him, he didn't even look cute enough to get with. He damn sure looked more like a junkie than I had as a crackhead at that point. *"Nah homie, I'm good,"* I said. He tried to convince me and I refused giving him my number so we could link up later. Just like that, he got up and moved on. I never saw him again, but that just got my wheels turning. How was I gonna get that next hit when I got out with no money and no job? I knew I wasn't going back to the hotel. I had no desire, especially after my kids were taken. What was I working for? They could take my apartment and everything at that point. I was sure my eviction was coming soon since I had stopped paying my rent. And I better not even try to ask my mom for more of my inheritance money. I only had a few days left in there, so I had to figure out a plan. Me and my plans. I was gonna make something happen though. I always did.

The day of my release came and I got my cell phone back. I put my plan in motion. The facility gave me a bus pass to get home. I never used it, nor did I call Stan to pick me up because I had a plan he would've thrown a monkey wrench in. Instead, I called another guy friend, a former co-worker from one of my temp jobs, to come pick me up. I gave him a sob story about how I didn't have any money and I needed a ride home. I don't remember if I told him I was there for my drug addiction, which I was ashamed of back then, or my alcohol addiction. Most likely the latter. Reluctantly, he said he would pick me up. I waited for him away from the recovery center nearer to the bus stop. He came and got me and riding in his truck, my plan was still in motion. Sob story number two. I asked him for pocket money. I explained I had stopped working to go into the rehab so I didn't have any more checks waiting for me when I got home and it would be a while before I would have any money again. All I needed was pocket money for emergencies to hold me over, I said, even if it was only 10 dollars. He reluctantly gave me some cash when he dropped me off. And that, ladies and gents, was how I got my next hit. As soon as I got into my apartment, I called my dealer. I was happy to be back home to get another hit. I couldn't wait. Rehab didn't do sh!t for me.

That first hit after having been off the drug for a while will have you floating on clouds. Previously, out of habit in my apartment, I would either smoke in my bedroom or if too many people were around messing with my high, I would smoke in my bathroom. Always away from the eyes of my kids. Out of habit, I went straight to the bathroom to make my pipe and light up, even though my bedroom was empty and available when I got home. I don't know why I chose the bathroom that day.

Was it the next day or a few days later I called my dealer again? Time was of no essence to me. I don't remember if he said he was out of what I wanted at the time or that it would be a while until he could bring it to me or he didn't answer his phone. Regardless, I had to call a backup in my phone, someone I never copped from before. I didn't even remember the name. It just said "backup dealer." I don't remember who gave me his number or how I got it, but he said he definitely knew who I was when I gave him my address. I got what I needed and went back in the bathroom. Took that first hit and I remember feeling like, *"Oh sh!t I'm way out of control. Something ain't right. I gotta sit down on the toilet."* It was a different feeling that I had never felt before, not even my first time ever using.

I woke up lying on the floor, prone position, eyes adjusting to the dark. I saw my pipe laying next to me. I had no clue what time it was or how long I had been lying there. I knew it was daylight when I started smoking but the bathroom window showed it was dark outside. It was darkness all around me. I hadn't turned on my lights earlier. I tried to get up. My legs wouldn't let me. I tried again. Nothing. I could not move. I did not have enough strength to get up. Finally, I was able to lift up on my arms and literally drag myself out of the bathroom. A slow drag. One arm after the other. The whole time I was thinking, *"What is wrong with my legs? Why can't I get up and walk?"* I was panicking. *"I need to call someone for help. I need to call Stan! O my God, I need to get to my phone."* My phone was in my bedroom, so I continued to drag myself.

I got myself to the hallway between the bathroom and my bedroom. For whatever reason, I could not tell you why, I flipped over on my back and laid there, exhausted from trying to move myself around, instead of staying in the prone position I was already in. Then I heard it...a man's voice. I got scared and panicked, "Oh sh!t someone's in my apartment. That's not Stan's voice. How did this man get in? Did I leave my door unlocked? Am I being robbed? Was I about to be raped again?" All that in a millisecond flashed through my mind. Then I heard another voice...My deceased dad's voice. He and that other man's voice, and it sounded like they were standing right behind my head. The two men were going back and forth. Man: *"We have to get her to the hospital."* Dad: *"No, I got her."* I heard my dad's voice and I cried out to him...*"Daddy, Daddy, Daddy... help me."* I was saying it so long and drawn out, like I had trouble speaking. But I know for a fact I said it out loud. It was not in my thoughts. I was hearing them speak out loud also. I've had hallucinations before while I was high with hearing and sight, and for sure this was not like the others. I tried to turn my head around to see him, but I was paralyzed. I literally could not move or turn my head around. Dad: *"I'm right here. I got you."* Man: *"She needs help, we gotta take her."* Dad: *"No leave her right here. I got her."* They kept going back and forth, my dad's voice getting more defiant. I couldn't hear the rest of what they were saying because at that point, I was crying so hard because my dad was right there, within arms reach, but I couldn't turn to see him. It had been four years since he died and all I wanted was to see him and touch him. Whatever the two men said in the end, my dad won. The other voice left and my dad said to me, *"Don't worry. I'm here."* My arm finally lifted off the floor. I tried to reach my hand back behind my head to touch him or for him to touch my hand. I tried to turn my head to see him, but my head still wouldn't move. All I heard was words fading away, like he was flying away, dissolving in the wind. I could hear him but couldn't make out the words. Then he was gone and I was in silence. The last thing I heard was not to worry, he was there with me. But he wasn't. He was gone. And all I did was lay there and sob, sob, sob.

Eventually, I turned back over and this time was able to half crawl, half drag myself to my room. I lifted myself onto the bed with my upper body strength and reached across for my cordless house phone. Phone in hand, I started feeling like my chest was gonna bust. It was beating so hard and fast. I was short of breath and getting weak again. I was thinking I was gonna die, right there where I laid. I had no one around to help me. It never dawned on me to dial 911. I don't know why. Was I too ashamed? Was I still mad at the police because they helped take my kids away from me? I really don't know. But what I do know is that I tried to call Stan. I just wanted my friend to help me not die, not right there, not right then, and not like that. I tried but my mind was in such a panic that I was dying and in a fog that I could not for the life of me remember his number. Then I thought to just scroll through the contacts until I landed on his name. I didn't remember how to scroll through my contacts or the call log. I was pressing all the wrong buttons. Nothing was getting me to his name. I was a mess. My mind was a mess. I could think of what I wanted to do, but my brain was too foggy to remember how to do it. Any other time I scrolled through the log like nothing. That time I couldn't figure out how to scroll. I was frustrated and scared at the same time. I was crying AGAIN in between gasping and my chest hurting. I pulled the spiral notebook off my nightstand and with my eyes adjusted to the dark, I wrote a note. *"If anyone finds me dead and this letter, tell my kids I love them and I'm sorry."* I wrote some more that I can't remember. That was the gist of the letter to my kids with something like, *"Whoever keeps them, please raise them together. Please don't separate them"* cuz they had two different fathers. How could I remember to write words but not make a phone call? Good question. Then I laid back in my bed and closed my eyes, still crying and praying to God: *"Let this feeling go away. I don't want to die. But if I die, please take me to Heaven. I didn't mean any harm to anyone. I'm so sorry, God."*

I woke up and looked around. I don't know how long I was asleep again. It was still dark. The phone, pen, and notebook were next to me. I finally lifted up. I thought, *"I'm alive! Thank God! I made it to wake up!"* I read over my death note and pushed it aside. I could barely make it out, so whoever would have found it probably wouldn't have understood because it wasn't legible. I got up from the bed and could walk again, like nothing happened with my legs not working earlier. I went straight into my living room, turned on the lights, grabbed my Bible off of the radio bookcase, and sat on the couch. It was the same Bible that I would follow along in when Tasha would read to me all those nights. Well, it would be open and she would read. I'd be so high, I really didn't follow along. I just listened to her voice until I fell asleep. I never even remembered what books in the Bible she read from. This time my mind seemed clear, so I prayed to God that He would tell me what scripture I needed to read at that moment. I asked that He would guide my fingers, as I opened the pages, to find what He wanted me to read. I was thinking, *"Once I open this Bible, I will probably be scrolling through pages not understanding anything."* But I was ready to pull an all-nighter until I found what gave me peace, the same way I had scoured thousands of scriptures until I found the perfect one for my daddy's obituary. So there I was, ready to scour the pages.

I opened my Bible to a random page. It was pre-marked to a page in Psalms that fell open. There was a small piece of paper stuck in between those pages, a note from my son. My

6-year-old baby boy. It said, "*Mommy I (drawing of a heart) you.*" I never remembered the note. Did he give it to me and I stuck it in there? Or did he stick it in there, hoping I would find it? Either way, I was surprised. Then I realized I missed my babies so much. I was bawling again. Tears and snot. How many times within the last month had I cried for them? My goodness. I wiped my face and looked down where the small piece of paper lay. There. Right there. **Psalm 71**. I read it over and over and over and over again. It was speaking to me. It gave me peace. As I was reading, there was a knock on my door. I get up to answer it. WOW! Someone who I had kicked out even before I had cleaned house with everyone else (another story for another day) was there, begging me to come in to smoke her crack. She needed a safe place to smoke. If I told you the story about how she and I got into it. Yeah, two crackheads out in the middle of the street acting a fool, ready to fight. We were wildin' in them streets. Anyway, I told her no. She begged and begged, then paused. She held up the baggie and offered me a rock for her to come in to smoke. Wow! I had no—absolutely no—desire. I told her no again. She looked at me crazy and said it was free. Why wouldn't I want the free rock? She was right. In any other circumstance, I would have taken it in a heartbeat. But at that moment, I looked at her in disgust and said, "*No*" one last time, and slammed the door in her face. I truly believe she thought it had to do with us falling out over the BS in the street. But all I know is at that moment, I felt peace, and I didn't want that feeling to leave me. I know now the devil brought that to me. He doesn't come dressed in red with horns and a pitchfork, but with the desires of your heart. All of a sudden...free drugs? But there were a couple more times after that. Other people would come and try to smoke in my apartment and give me freebies for access into my place. Each of them was surprised when I said no, just like the first time.

I never went back to reading the Bible that night after I was interrupted, but I called Tasha. My ace, who was always there for me, wherever and whenever. I had no recollection of the time, but I'm sure it had to be the middle of the night after the whole day's ordeal with me falling out and it being dark out when I came to, and trying to walk, and writing my death note to anyone who would find me dead. Of course, she answered. I told her about passing out and waking up to my dad being there but I couldn't see him because I couldn't turn my head. She assured me I had a supernatural experience. She never made fun of me or judged me. She was just there for me, her addict friend, as always. And that's why I love her. But I've never had a supernatural encounter before, so I was skeptical. She knew that's what it was because she said she's had them herself. And although that was my first, it wasn't my last supernatural experience. As I began my walk in Christ, I've had a few more encounters that I will share in later chapters.

Can you believe the one and only thing that actually stopped my drug desires was me reading the Word for myself? Psalm 71 saved me, along with the angels God had placed around me and the prayers of everyone. Psalm 71 sparked something in my spirit and soul. All the times I prayed to God to help me quit and He finally did, on His time, through His Word. Not me on my own, not through rehab, and not from Tasha or anyone else reading the Bible to me. I'm sure some of it helped. I'm sure the prayers of my mom, friends, and other family members who wished to see me clean were all heard too, because I do believe in the power of prayer. I had a whole village that never ceased praying for me, but God wanted me to seek Him through His Word for myself. I know that rehab does work for some. I only tried it one time and didn't give it my all, and that didn't do it for me. Sometimes it takes one or more stints in rehab to get it right. God has multiple resources for different people to be delivered from all types of addictions. He delivered me from crack, but I still had an addiction to alcohol, which I will address in a later chapter. But by the grace of God, He healed me of my drug addiction. As of 2023, I've been clean 19 years. My clean date is October 2004.

    I went from sniffing coke to being a straight crackhead. I had burnt lips from the crack pipes, and black fingers from excessive lighter flickering, the unkempt hair, baggy clothes falling off my small and frail body frame, and probably was even smelly because I barely remember taking showers during that time. While I was in my drug addiction, I thought I kept myself up, but I know now I was looking like a hot mess to everyone else. My place went from the party place to the crack house. Many untold adult stories happened there around my small children. I remember a few times when the kids were asleep, at least I hope they were, I would go into their bedroom they shared and smoke in their closet, just to hide from the others in my house smoking. That way I wouldn't have people begging me to share my pieces with anyone or have others messing with my high. At two different times, I had two different women living with us in our home. People were stealing from me, stealing from my children. There are all sorts of other and worse things my children probably witnessed. Many of the drug people I ran with and allowed into my space and my home have died. Why am I still here? Why has God spared my life once again? Nothing I am boasting about, but giving God His accolades and glory and sharing my testimony. These are my truths I had to acknowledge and come to terms with. The guilt and shame I once had, I have no more.

I only realize now that I ran out of money just at the time of my deliverance, after my kids were taken and after I came back from rehab. Two people had given me money to get back on my feet and for "emergencies," but I used it both times for more drugs. I say "just in time" because after I fell out and quit drugs, how else would I have gotten money after that for my habit? I don't believe I ever hit my rock bottom by that time because I know things could've and would've gotten worse for me from there to support my habit. Believe me, it was coming. But I got clean, right when my money ran out. Only by the GRACE OF GOD!!! Ya heard me!!!

That one-time dealer I copped from that last time, I have no idea what was in those rocks he sold me that knocked me out. But what was meant for evil knocked sense into me that night. Enough sense for me to pick up my Bible and read.

I hadn't heard from my mom in a while. The last time was when the officers told me to let baby daddy take them to her and she was on the phone. Other than friends Tasha, Regina, and Stan, I didn't hear from anyone else during that time. But from the time I quit smoking, my mind was clearing and I was on my road to recovery. I started answering all my phone calls again. I stopped hiding and had to get back into the real world. My two older cousins, who are sisters, Tradean and Jean, had heard from my mom about what was going on and Zakiya found out. From that day on, they would all call and check on me from time to time and give me some encouragement. Not just then but still, 19 years later, those same six still call and visit me to check on me and the kids to make sure I'm still good, that we're good. Those six are forever indebted in my heart. During my recovery in North Carolina, they had no idea how much their reaching out meant to me. It gave me so much hope, and I felt so much love from people who were outside my circle of people. Even Ms. Bo came back around me, even without my kids being there, to make sure I was good and to get me out of the house to be around her family from time to time. She also never gave up on me, and she had only known me for a short time. The kids always remembered her. She was their safe haven when I wasn't.

Good ole Stan...He was so proud of me. He introduced me to Terri, a female friend of his who he trusted to be my AA sponsor when I got clean. She invited me to her church and all kinds of wholesome activities and events. Then he introduced me to his family, his *real* family. His ex-wife and all his grown daughters, sons, and grandkids. He took me around them a couple of times, and I spent time with them at their homes. I asked him why he would include me like that. He said I was good people and they were too, and he wanted me to be around positive people. They weren't judgmental about my recent past or anything because he, in fact, was a recovering addict. So they knew exactly how to connect with me. They showed me so much love, and I was honored to be received into the Diggs' crew. To this day, I still speak with his ex-wife and one of his daughters. I am so grateful for Stan. He looked out for me up until the day I left North Carolina to go back to New York City.

During the time of my recovery, I had to get back in good graces with my broadcasting school. My graduation would be coming up in a few months, and I wanted to be ready. I spoke with the president of the school again, and she said she would have all of my professors give me extra work to make up for missed time. Not only did I have to make up my original work, but they had me write extra essays and do some extra-credit work. That was all fine for me. I was excited to get my life back in order. I had a lot of hands-on equipment experience, i.e., running sound boards, voice-overs, running cameras, and editing done at the school's inside set-up studio and the local gospel radio station they had us train at, WDEX 1430 AM, before I left to go to rehab. When I got delivered and clean off drugs, I landed an internship at PBS (WTVI TV42) in Charlotte. All I did was run cameras there but boy, it was a start. I was super excited! I was doing something my heart desired for so many years, to work behind the scenes in television broadcasting or in the film industry.

During that time, I told everyone I spoke to that once I graduated, I would be moving back up to New York. Very few people knew my story about my kids being "stolen" from me or knew I was going back to show my mom I was clean so that I could get my children back. The majority just assumed I was moving back to start my broadcasting career with my new degree. But for sure, I was going to get my kids back.

As graduation neared, I got antsy about going. I didn't go to my high school graduation, nor the prom, nor the senior trip. I just wanted out back then. I'm not built for the extra fuss that goes with it. I didn't graduate with my peers because one, I was in a new school, my third high school, and didn't know anyone and two, I was in my last and fifth year because of my truancies. I was a year behind and all my peers had graduated the year before. I was late, so what did I care in high school? I didn't try to get to know anyone. I was pretty much a loner and just wanted to finish school. I just wanted the diploma and to be done.

So no graduation again. This time, it was a small class and I didn't want all eyes on me, especially with them knowing I was coming out of rehab. But again, I'm not all about the fuss. So I told them I would not be attending the graduation. The president tried her hardest to convince me to attend the dinner, saying she would give me my degree there. I still politely declined. But on my graduation day, what did I do? I bought myself a graduation card and signed it with an encouraging message to myself, then thanked God for seeing me through to the end of the course. I FREAKIN MADE IT! It wasn't easy, but I made it to the finish line! I cried so many happy tears. I was so proud of myself that day. Extremely proud because the entertainment industry was in my blood from when I was a little girl. I even took film studies at Bronx Community College back in 1996-1998 but never finished because I dropped out a little while after I had my first son in 1997. So this was a life-long dream of mine to be in the industry. This was just the beginning. I was stoked! But I never told anyone I graduated, never called anyone, never celebrated it with anyone. This was just for me. Just me and my card, alone in my apartment. No one knew the day I completed broadcasting school except my classmates and the president, who dropped by my apartment on her way to the graduation dinner to hand me my degree in person. That was in 2004 and to this day, I still have my graduation card.

I saw my girl Regina a few more times and spent time with Stan and the new people he introduced me to who kept me uplifted and encouraged. And true to my word, I made my way back to the Bronx. The good ole boogie down. I made it back home. That was the last of Charlotte, North Carolina, for me.

I had a lot of rough days there but I left with a degree, a TV internship, and a promising future. All I had to do was get my kids back because what was life without them? They were all I had. It was us against the world, and I had to get us back together again.

10
THE BAHAMAS

The LORD is my light and my salvation; whom shall I fear? the LORD is the strength of my life; of whom shall I be afraid? When the wicked, even mine enemies and my foes, came upon me to eat up my flesh, they stumbled and fell.

Psalm 27:1-2 (KJV)

I went back up to New York. With my broadcasting degree, I landed another internship at FOX 5NY at the assignment editor's desk in Manhattan. That was my official position, but I also was a field producer trainee who went out with the cameramen to interview subject matter experts and get small clips and footage for the station every now and then. Simultaneously, I stayed with my mom for a while throughout my next pregnancy and up until I had my third baby. True to her word, she allowed me to take back control of my first two kids she was taking care of. When my new baby boy was three months old, I moved down to Columbus, Georgia. My now three children and I stayed in one of the many houses my cousin owned. Why? The same reason I always moved us out of New York, to give my kids a better life. By that time, I had moved us from the Bronx, New York, to Charlotte, North Carolina once, back to New York, down to Spartanburg, South Carolina, back again to Charlotte, again to New York, and finally to Columbus. As I got older and wiser, I realized trouble finds you wherever you are. No place is better than the next. It's all in how you make the best of where you're at with what you have.

I got a call in Georgia from a male stripper living in New York who I gave my number to, the last time I was up there, at a friend's bachelorette party cuz he wouldn't take no for an answer after his show. Chocolate Thunder was his stage name, but I called him by his real name. For this story, I'll call him C.T. I was never interested in him because he was so cocky. I gave him my number so he would get out of my face and leave me alone. He literally hounded me and said he wasn't gonna let up until I gave him my number. I don't know why I didn't just give him a fake number. I was used to giving out fake names and numbers if I wasn't interested. If anybody knows about the 5411s, you know what I'm talking about, lol. That was our go-to last four digits to any made-up number. It came from the price of the high-top Reebok sneakers females wore. That was the style back then. But for whatever reason, he got my real name and real number. I literally ignored him while he was performing. I was in the kitchen eating while everybody was having fun with him in the living room. But he came looking for me and took the plate out of my hand and walked me back into the living room with everybody so he could finish performing on me. I remember I and another girl were the ones to open the door when he came in. He came to find me after he changed in another room and went in the living room to perform and didn't see me there with the other girls. I never even met up with him after he got my number and called me when I was still living in New York. I had been avoiding him. But this call was different. It wasn't just to meet up with him. It was to go on a trip with him to the Bahamas. First I said no, but my cousins convinced me to take the free trip and my aunt Debra said she would watch my three kids. It was a very short trip so I thought, *"Why not? It'll be quick anyway."* But I was very hesitant and very skeptical. He called me out of the blue and we never saw each other after the bachelorette party, so why me? I figured he paid for the trip and whoever he was supposed to take wasn't going anymore, so he was just going down the line calling everybody until somebody said yes. Those were my thoughts then and still are today.

So yayyy, free trip for me! Woohoo! He bused me up on the Greyhound to meet up with him at Port Authority, New York. We waited a day and then flew to the Bahamas together. I'm thinking, *"This will be fun."* But I should've stuck to my first instinct and not gone because I wasn't interested in him, and you know what happens when you get a free trip. They expect you to have sex with them for payment. Anyway, things went left very quickly. We were only there for two nights and three days, but what a disaster.

It started with him being obnoxiously demanding and controlling about my hair in the Greyhound station, specifically, about the scarf on my head. But who was gonna be sleeping all those hours on their head to mess up their hair? From Georgia to New York? Certainly not me. Well... red flag number one. I'm so sure, as a stripper, he was used to having his way with the ladies, just like the ladies were throwing themselves at him at the bachelorette party where they were giving me mean looks because he kept trying to get my number instead of theirs. On the phone he was so sweet, but what a 180 in the terminal. So it started before we even got on the flight to make it to our destination.

We didn't talk on the flight there. Another red flag. Once we landed, things only got worse. But the resort, which I'm declining to name for specific purposes, was beautiful. We got to our room and immediately he told me we were going to the casino. I'm definitely not a casino girl but I figured we could go because we had more time and days to do other things, right? I thought we'd get the casino out the way. It was his trip, so I thought we could do what he wanted initially.

There was minimum talking on the way to the casino. Once inside, he looked around for a minute and went over to "his" table with me following behind him like a lost puppy. He played for a while, the whole time winning and the whole time ignoring me like I wasn't there. Never once did he look at me, and he definitely didn't speak to me at all. No one would have known we were there together, even with me standing right behind him. I was getting tired and impatient but he was winning big, being a player, loud, flashy, and cocky, having laughs and talking with the others around him, still totally ignoring me. So I took a few steps back because ugghhhh...I just couldn't. I decided to walk around to waste time, going out to the lobby and window-shopping the stores down the corridors. I went back after a while and looked at ole boy who had been ignoring me. He was surrounded by white women giggling over him and showing him so much winning attention. He was laughing and talking with them. Everybody was just flirting all over the place. I stayed for a few minutes to see if he would actually look my way, but nope. I was good and couldn't care less, but was also disgusted at the same time. *So now you're showing other females attention like I'm not here with you?"* Whether I cared about being there with him or not was not the issue. The level of disrespect that I don't tolerate was the issue. I looked one last time and headed back to our room.

It was still daylight out. I watched TV and ordered room service. By the time he came in, it was the middle of the night and he was sloppy drunk. He pulled thousands of dollars out of his pockets and was mumbling some stuff I barely understood. But I did make out that he had won a lot of that money that night. Then he proceeded to put that, his wallet, and his watch in the safe, the whole time cursing me out. He told me not to be trying to watch him for the code. I thought, *"Boy, if you don't go on about yourself! I give zero f^&ks about you or whatever you have going on. I'm definitely not no thief or materialistic. I don't want nothing you got going on."* I was just disgusted. Not once did he come try to look for me to make sure I was ok that whole day after I left. But it was all good. I was fine in my own peace in the room alone. All we did was argue back and forth about nothing. He was cursing me out and I was cursing him right back about nothing! To him, I wanted his money. Paranoia maybe? Because I'm sure all the women he was used to wanted his stripper money, but I was not the one. I could play the game, but I was always a chick who didn't want any guy for his money. During the back and forth, he was drunk and talking too much and confessed he was at the table all night, winning big. He got in the bed, pushed up on me to have sex, and of course that was another fight. He ignored me ALL DAY! From the airport down to the casino, and then it was the middle of the night/next day. And he thought he was getting some? My refusing him drew out the arguing and tugging and pushing even longer. Eventually, he fell asleep, and I got my a%# out of the room quick.

The Angels Are Watching

I went downstairs to the front desk to ask about pushing my flight up to...NOW! I wanted to sneak out and fly back immediately. I told the receptionist that I was willing to pay any extra fees. I was so ready to leave his a%#. He wouldn't care and neither would I. I wanted to ghost him and never speak to him again. She tried to help me but said there were no flights going out until our third day there, and that was the day we were going back anyway. So I was stuck. I took my sorry a%# back up to my room and got into the bed like nothing ever happened. He never woke up anyway, he was drunk sleep.

Almost noon on day number two, he rolled over and tried to have sex againnnn. Bruh nah! Nope! You not getting nada from me. But he was real aggressive with it, so we were really tugging back and forth. I was thinking, *"This man is really gonna rape me. Here I go again. Always putting myself in these situations."* The first time I was really naïve. This time I knew what I was getting myself into. I even planned beforehand to give him some on the trip. But unless he made up big time for the day before, that would never happen. He was all about himself, that selfish, cocky, arrogant bastard! And after his shenanigans that first day, he was getting nothing! So he relented, got up, showered, and left the room. He did not say a word to me. I showered and left thinking, *"I'm cool by myself. I'll go down to the bar and chill for a while."* But instead of going to the inside lobby bar, I decided to walk to the outside pool and just chill in the lounge chair. It was beautiful and huge outside. And lo and behold, who do I see there in the water? C.T. and two white girls. They were giggling and touching each other, him lifting them up and throwing them around in the water. Then one put her arms around his neck and held onto him. I'm not sure if they were the same two from the previous night but I would bet my bottom dollar they were. I was like, "*Damn. Just f^&k me again.*" As I walked around the pool to get over to the other side where I saw the dry bar, he and the chicks started swimming toward the pool bar inside the water. He saw me and briefly stopped, but then kept going. "*Ok, so you just not gonna speak? Cool.*" At that point, no one even knew he came with somebody. He could've gone on the trip himself. I was not having fun and was ready to go home since yesterday.

I walked over to the bar, sat, ordered my drink, and started sipping alone by myself. Then this Black female about my age came out of nowhere and started talking to me. She said she came solo. It was her birthday trip and the girls who were supposed to come with her canceled, so she didn't want to waste her money. That struck a red flag for me but I couldn't place it. I felt uneasy for a quick second, but decided to believe her story and we continued talking. I told her about being out there with C.T. but basically, we were separated and I wasn't having any fun. That's when she invited me out. She said we should go to this club and was hyping it up. I asked how she knew so much about it. She told me it wasn't her first time there at the resort. "*Hmmm...,*" I thought. Now that part comes out. Another red flag. She said she liked it so much before, she booked it for her birthday trip. I believed her. I asked how we would get to the club. She said she would call us a taxi and ask for the limo instead. She said she knew the driver and he would not even charge us. I believed her. We decided on a time to get dressed and meet back downstairs in the front. I was excited to finally be doing something fun on my last night in the Bahamas.

I went back up, ordered room service and ate, then got ready for my night while sipping. Not once did C.T. come to the room. Not to check on me or for anything in general. I put my makeup on and was out. I didn't care about him. I was gonna make my last night count, with or without him.

I met the girl out in front. I don't remember her name. I'm sure it was a fake name anyway. Then we waited for a while and a car pulled up, but it wasn't a limo. The guy said something about why he didn't have the limo. I didn't understand what he was saying, with his heavy accent, but I didn't care, she understood him. Actually, I was excited about the limo ride, as I had never been in one before except for my dad's funeral, and that doesn't count. As long as we had a way to the club, I was good. I was sipping and feeling nice. I just didn't want to sit in the room alone. I wanted to take back a report to my cousins that I got something out of the trip.

We went through all these narrow dirt roads. I was like, *"What was all this?"* I went to the islands on a cruise before but never went through where the locals lived, so this was new to me. It was starting to get dark out and all those rocky and narrow roads started to scare me. After what seemed like forever, we pulled up in front of a rinky dink-looking shack. *"Huh? What the…? You sure this is the right place?"* I asked before we got out. She said, *"Yes."* We went in and lo and behold, it was a strip club.

Inside, about two songs were played before they said they were closing. I think it was about 10-ish, and I only had one drink there. We stayed until they were shutting down. Apparently ole girl knew the people in there and introduced me to the owner and a few stripper girls. Red flag. But I was chill. They were so hyped to talk to me, a girl from New York. They wanted my number. I refused. So they all gave me their numbers and said to keep in touch because they wanted to visit New York one day. I threw away the numbers once I got home to Georgia. I figured I would never see them again. The

The Bahamas

owner explained to me that they closed early if they didn't have any customers. I understood that cuz it was empty inside. I told the girl that I was still ready to party and we needed to find another club cuz one thing I didn't like was wasting my drinks, a good outfit, and makeup to go nowhere. The guy told us about a regular club, not a strip club, close to there. I was hyped about it but ole girl told me she had something better for us. I believed her. She called and we waited for our taxi. A different driver showed up.

Inside the car, I thought she was going to take me to a different club the owner guy told us about. But instead, she said she copped some coke and wanted us to go back to her room to sniff. Whoa! What? My first thought was she must've gotten it from the club we just left, unbeknownst to me, or it could've been from the first cab driver she "knew so well." My second thought was how she just assumed I was a cokehead, of all drugs. Most strangers would offer weed to someone they didn't know, but coke? I never once mentioned anything to her about me doing drugs in my past. My third thought was, *"Well, it's not crack. So yea, I'll be alright. I can do coke with her."* I agreed and we went to her room in our hotel but on a lower floor than my room.

We got to her room a little after midnight. I knew I had to leave to fly back to the States later that day, but I still had some time to chill. I was excited to sniff again. It had been a while. I have no doubt that brief desire was the devil once again tempting me to return to my wicked ways.

In her room, she went in the bathroom. She came out naked and got in the bed under the sheets. Mind blown! I was sitting at the foot on the other side of her bed. She was talking to me, but I had no idea what she was saying. I was thinking, *"Why is she naked?"* I finally looked at her. She had the coke in her hand

and told me to get undressed and get under the sheets with her so we could *"have some fun."* I didn't see where she had pulled the coke from but there it was in her hand all of a sudden, and I wanted some. Ole satan was pulling on me hard to backslide. So I told her I wanted to use the bathroom to freshen up. In the bathroom, I was still thinking, *"What gave her the impression I used to sniff?"* I didn't remember any conversation that whole day that implied that. Back then I didn't speak about my drug habits except to those who knew me, and only if they asked me questions about it, but definitely not to a random stranger. And what impression did I give to imply that I was with a girl before cuz she was just butt naked! I was very confused. But there I was, contemplating life once again. Yup, I was gonna go back out to the room and have some fun. The whole trip was a bust, so I deserved some fun. And fun wasn't just with the drugs. There was other "fun" involved—fun I hadn't had since I was younger, running the streets, having threesomes and orgies, and such.

My spirit slowed down my excitement. I started to get scared, not to start using drugs again, but something about that girl started to scare me. I felt so uneasy and uncomfortable and I didn't know why. I could not place it. I walked out of the bathroom fully clothed and told her I was going back up to my room. The look on her face dropped and she sat up. She kept asking me why. She wanted to know what was wrong and asked me not to leave, to stay and have a drink. I had no answers. I just kept saying I wanted to go back to my room. She had this very puzzled look as I left. My heart was so afraid, and I didn't know why. As I reflect on the moment, I am convinced the Holy Spirit was speaking within me and gave me the power to avoid temptation. God's angels protected me from making bad decisions and putting myself in danger.

The Bahamas

Back upstairs finally, I was relieved I was alone because C.T. wasn't there. I figured he was out with his new white chicks, so I went to sleep. Then there was banging on the door. I sat up, scared. Who the hell was banging in the middle of the night? I went to the door like the G I was... yeah right, lol. I was shook. I swung it open hard and mad, then realized it wasn't really banging but more like C.T. was fumbling to swipe his key card, but he wasn't alone. The two women were with him, trying to hold him up while he was fumbling with the door. When I swung it open, they looked at me very surprised. Then one of them said, *"Oh, I didn't know someone was in here."* I said, very nasty, *"Yeah, I'm here. He's not on this trip alone."* I wasn't sure if they really knew about me and was playing it off. I couldn't care less. They were stuttering and trying to explain that they were bringing him back to his room safely because he was drunk, as I could clearly tell. That was his MO the whole short trip—gambling and getting drunk. I said, *"I got him"* and dragged him in, and they still tried to come in. I slammed the door on them so hard. What did they think? That I was going to let them in with him? I was cursing them out in my head and cursing him out at the same time. The nerve of all of them!!! I didn't get him all the way to the bed. He was too heavy for me and slumped to the floor halfway to the bed, mumbling drunk talk, nothing that I understood. I went in his pockets and pulled out his wallet in one pocket and all the cash in the other pocket—thousands and thousands of dollars I assumed because I didn't count it. But it was a lot of bills like I had never seen in my whole life before. I said to myself, *"He must've been in the casino all day again, winning big again."* And it was more than the last time. I was about to put it on the dresser but went over to the safe and saw it was ajar. I just sat everything in there and went back to bed. I thought to lock it but then decided not to at the last minute. I didn't close it all the way, just ajar so it looked closed and he was still on the floor. What good did it do to stay unlocked? I don't know.

Then there was more knocking on the door. I screamed, "*Who is it?*" I could hear the women talking, saying something. I walked closer to the door and a man started talking, saying he was checking on his "friend" he met downstairs at the bar in the lobby where they were hanging out. "*Oh, so now he was making more friends there?*" They all wanted to make sure he was ok because he seemed pretty drunk. They wanted me to let them in so they could make sure he was ok. I started yelling and cursing them out through the door. I never saw what the man looked like, but I was scared!!! I was thinking, "*What if they were coming in to try to rob him?*" I really didn't care about him, but I damn sure cared about me. I'm thinking, "*These strangers don't mean this guy no good.*" I was already in there taking care of him. I mean, I really wasn't. But at least he was safe with me. So what else could they do for him? I really don't think they expected someone to be in his room. So, I'm sure they had other plans for him, and it didn't involve making sure he was ok. I screamed at them through the door and threatened to call the front desk if they didn't leave. That was the last I heard of them. I didn't go back to sleep the rest of the night. I was scared as sh!t, thinking they were gonna come through the door and rob us, although I had nothing, so really rob C.T. of all that money that he won. And there we were in a foreign country. It all seemed sketchy. Meanwhile, I was looking around to see what I could use as a weapon if they got through the door before I could get security up there. If push came to shove, I would have to lock the safe. There I was protecting somebody who clearly didn't give any f^&ks about me. But there I was, doing what I do out of loyalty because that's just who I am.

The Bahamas

The rest of the night was silent. C.T. slept on the floor the next couple of hours. When he got up, he asked where his money was. That was his very first question. I told him everything that happened overnight. He counted his money and decided to finally talk to me with some respect. He never thanked me, but nonetheless spoke to me with decency and how it was good of me that I took him in and left everybody out. He talked about how I put his stuff in the safe, even though I didn't lock it, and was even surprised at how I didn't try to rob him and take any of his money myself. Whatever, dude! Like what kind of chicks did he really mess with? He was drunk, so I'm pretty sure he didn't remember exactly how much money he had won anyway. But that was the end of our decent conversation because after that, we got ourselves ready in silence and rode back to the airport in silence. I don't remember us hugging or even saying goodbye before we parted in the airport. I flew straight to Georgia and him to New York. That was the last I ever heard from him. He never called to check that I got back safely or anything, but it didn't bother me. I was good not hearing from him.

As the years went on, I later realized three things from that trip. The first was from a movie I had watched. I don't remember the name of the movie back then but it was definitely about card counting and scamming. Bingo! I remembered he had mentioned something one time when he was drunk mumbling, but I didn't pay it any mind because I didn't understand what that all meant. Later I understood that was what the short little trip was about in the Bahamas. Get in and get out. Don't draw too much attention. I don't know how well he did about the not drawing attention part but you know how the rest went.

The second realization from the movie was that I was supposed to be his arm candy to be a distraction for his scamming to make it look like he was on a vacation with his "girlfriend." I failed that part miserably, as we argued or barely talked at all throughout that three-day trip. He must have expected a female to do anything and everything he said, which he was used to as a stripper, and for me to look the part, sitting and standing pretty by him. But I never got that memo. I thought he invited me just to not waste his money that I figured he paid for someone else who pulled out of the trip. But I realized he probably used me for his own selfish gain at the casino. His original plan didn't work, the part about me being by his side the whole time, but he still went home with more money than he arrived with, and I didn't see one red cent.

The third thing I realized years later when social media started popping off was that what I was going to sniff with that girl could have been laced with something. I could have ended up dead or passed out, and she could've taken my room key and robbed us. Again, I had nothing of value to rob, but C.T. did. Had they been watching us? Her and her people? The white girls and their people? Was everybody in on it? I may be paranoid after the fact, but I just don't know. So many red flags I remember. I believe the Black girl who came up to me at the dry bar and said she had been there before. She probably lived out there and I fell for her lies. I don't remember her having an accent but she knew some people and how to get around. I don't know when, where, or how she got the drugs. I didn't see her sniff anything, but she was gonna give me some! I was really gonna be found dead or passed out naked with coke up my nose if my spirit didn't step in and scare me away. That was my angel's protection, had to be. Ain't no other way. I look back and see so much was wrong with that trip, and not just with C.T. I was so naïve. Instead of being mad that C.T. ruined my free trip, I should've been worried about my safety. There

The Bahamas

I went, traveling to unfamiliar territory and just frolicking about with strangers and the locals like I had no cares in the world. But how could I have possibly known back then? I had never heard of those deadly situations until years later when social media started putting them out into the world about people missing or dying while on vacation in another country.

I definitely gave everyone and everything the benefit of the doubt. We probably had all eyes on us from the time we stepped foot on that resort from every angle and there we were, separated the whole trip. Neither one of us was around to protect the other with the exception of that last night. That's exactly why they came after us. The Black girl with me and the white girls with him, with all his loud and flashy ways drawing attention to us. If I hadn't been in our room that last night, I don't know what would've happened to him. I don't know what would've happened to me if I had stayed in ole girl's room.

I thank God for sending His angels down to protect me yet again.

CHILD PROTECTIVE SERVICES

> *Truly I tell you, if you have faith as small as a mustard seed, you can say to this mountain, 'Move from here to there', and it will move. Nothing will be impossible for you.*
>
> **Matthew 17:20 (NIV)**

While still in Columbus, Georgia, I moved out of my cousin's house and had a little stint in the family shelter, House of Mercy. Nothing against the family I was with in Georgia, the Smiths, I just needed my own space to do my own thing with my own kids. My children and I have lived in numerous family shelters in different states. This shelter, by far, had the best standards for payment to live there, which was the requirement to attend Sunday church services and weekly Bible studies that were on location in their chapel. There was a children's daycare available during the services. My oldest two asked, on their own, to be baptized there. That was one of the greatest things about being there. After almost a year, we finally got into Chase Apartments, aka the projects, after being on the waitlist for months.

Child Protective Services

During that time, I landed a job at the local CCG-TV as a production assistant. What didn't I do there? Mike King, the station manager, made sure everyone who worked under him learned everything. Mike knew I hadn't done much producing or editing before at FOX 5 News or PBS, but he gave me a chance and trained me to be the best of the best. I assisted with production in the city council meetings, Newswatch programs, and all of the other local programs we ran at the station. He had me producing, writing, directing, and editing for segments. I was working cameras, prompters, soundboards, editing chroma key graphics on the green screen...all of that! You couldn't tell your girl nothing! Life was great working at CCG-TV. Even though I was at the shelter, he never treated me any differently. Mike not only cared about his staff at work, he cared about our well-being and our lives at home. He always made sure my kids and I were good and not just me but everyone that worked under him. He had good leadership skills and was a great mentor to us all. I can't ever thank him enough for all he taught me in the broadcasting industry behind the scenes and also politicking with the big bosses, the mayor, major sports athletes, celebrities, and all to land the best interviews. He taught us all how it was to be done as a man who was versatile in his skills and had many resources.

When I finally moved with my three kids into the projects, he was just as happy for me as I was for myself. My family in Georgia, the Smiths–my uncle, aunt, and cousins–were also happy for us. So much happened in that apartment. Some good, some bad.

I have many, many, many stories of Child Protective Services (CPS) being called on me, always for nonsense. Mostly for some bogus story someone made up when they were mad at me and trying to get back at me. CPS was almost called on me in South

The Angels Are Watching

Carolina by a staff worker in the welfare office. CPS was called on me in New York twice and in Georgia twice. CPS. CPS. CPS. Actually, in Columbus, Georgia, CPS is called DFCS. So I know, depending on your region, it's called CPS, DFCS, DYFS, etc. But the end result is the same. The protection of children against abuse and neglect—you get the idea. I always had a case going on with them. I could never shake them off my back and then, that same apartment was robbed. So much more had happened in that apartment, and my kids witnessed it all first-hand because they were directly involved in some of them. I don't know why so much happened in that apartment because if I remember correctly, I prayed over my home when we moved in, as I do every home I move into. But God has the last say on whatever He allows, and I don't need to know about or understand His reasons. As the Bible says in Proverbs, *Lean not unto my own understanding*. Whatever happened, He still made sure we were always safe. He made sure His angels were always watching.

One CPS case I want to talk about shows one of the many ways I struggled as a single parent and how it affected my children and me because I couldn't always afford necessities, such as medications.

CPS ALWAYS came after me for my kids for the wrong reasons. Before, with the drugs, I would understand the need but after the drugs, I really tried my best to live right and do the right things for my kids. But the devil had another agenda. It was like he knew where my weaker points were if he couldn't get me...Do. Not. Mess. With. My. Kids! CPS always ended up closing my cases, not finding me at fault, but I always cried to God, asking why He kept letting the devil come at me that way with them trying to take my kids when I was trying to raise them right and do the right thing. I know I wasn't perfect, but

Child Protective Services

I was not abusing or neglecting them. I was barely holding on to faith every time CPS came around. But then I would always pray and say to God, *"I have faith as small as a mustard seed,"* I would always put my two fingers close together, *"and I know You will keep me and my kids together because they are all I have in this world."* Me and them against the world, like I always told them. I realized I could always handle anything for myself and give lots of passes when it came to me as I grew up in the streets and was always in survival mode, but when the devil came at me through the way of my kids, he knew that was the ONLY way he could get at me and make me stressed out and worried. Nothing else could break me down more than anyone or anything messing with my kids. I WOULD FIGHT TIL THE DEATH OF ME! ON MY SOUL! For each and every one of them. There were lots of fights where I was defending my kids back then. Now, I'm learning to let God handle my battles. Well, most of them, I'm still a work in progress.

So I would pray, *"Please, God, don't let them take my kids away."* I prayed so hard. And I would tell God to back me up because He knew I meant well and was doing my best with my three kids by myself. I worked hard and sacrificed so much to keep us together. I was finally getting a child support check. After all the years of applying for child support, one of the kid's fathers decided to do the right thing. It was about $80 a month for one kid from one father. But thank God. That was better than the zero I had been getting for any of my kids all those years. I added that to my paychecks from the TV station, but I still wasn't making enough to sustain us. so I remained on food stamps and Medicaid for the four of us.

I was trying to keep up with life, working and running my household. I was in my late 20s with three small children in our new apartment. Our Medicaid lapsed before I renewed it, so I had to do the whole process over and reapply and had to wait until it was approved to use it again. When it rains, it pours. During the wait, my daughter ran out of her eczema topical medication creams, of course. Not one, but both medications and her school's nurse's office sent home a letter asking for more. First of all, the nurse's office had the only two we had. I really wished we had been approved for two of each because then I would've had one set at home and would have gladly sent it to the school. But no, that's not how it worked. So I sent a note back saying I was waiting for her Medicaid so I could get her some more because let's be honest, I couldn't afford them. One tube was $80 and the other $60. An extra $140??? That was not in my budget, especially back in those days. I barely carried a single dollar in my pocket for emergencies. Oooh, yes, times were rough for me.

So one day my daughter went to school and her eczema flared up. She was scratching her legs and ankle area, and they bled profusely. I got a phone call while at work telling me that she had been taken to the hospital. That's all they said. I left work to rush there. A Black woman and a Black man were standing there around her bed. I ignored them and talked straight to my daughter. I asked her if she was ok and what was wrong. Why was she there? She really didn't know what to say. She was a little girl and had no answers for me, but she was sitting up and breathing so I thought, "Thank God" she wasn't knocking on death's door, whatever the problem was. The female or male (I don't remember which one) asked me if I knew why they were there. I said no and I was about to ask who they were. I had assumed they were the doctor and nurse but after looking at them again, dressed in regular clothes, I thought they must've chaperoned her there from the school. No, they were from DFCS and there because they got

Child Protective Services

a call from the school saying it was a case of neglect because I failed to provide medication to the school for her condition. UGHHHHH!!!! WHY???? So I explained that I sent a letter to the nurse saying I was waiting for our Medicaid to go through again to get the medications because I did not have the money. I was upset, and I said *"Ya'll gonna take my kids because I can't afford her meds?"* I was kind of rude when I spoke, not because I meant to be but because I was scared that this time would be the time the devil would defeat me and have my kids taken. I felt such despair and anger at myself because, yet again, I couldn't provide for my kids the way I wanted to. Life was hard, and I was just trying to do my best. I wanted to cry right then and there, but I didn't. They said they understood and would close the case once I got the Medicaid and the medication and provided the proof to them. They left, and I took my daughter home. But before they closed my case, they passed it to a Black, arrogant male caseworker who abused his power and authority against me.

He pretty much knew my life story. I was a single mom and would do anything to keep my kids from being taken. Anything? I'm pretty sure anything at that point. I was not gonna lose them to not being able to afford my daughter's meds. Boy did he test the waters. He knew I didn't use my front door because it faced and led out to the Chattahoochee River, right outside our door, and my then two-year-old son couldn't swim. I taught the oldest two to always use the back door. I was very afraid to use my front door, and I told him so. And what did he do every visit? He went through the front just because he knew I wouldn't object when he knocked on the door. What was I supposed to do? Not answer? Not let him in? Then he would say I declined his visit to check on the kids. He already violated me, but I was intimidated by him having the authority to take my kids, so I kept letting it slide even though he irked me. He was not considerate at all and portrayed himself as more of an a%#hole. He gave me written homework that I had to add on to all the other things I had to do as a single parent and talked to me in condescending ways ALL THE TIME because I was a single Black female living in the projects. My place was always clean, but he would look around to find something he considered wrong. Anything. The dishes would be clean and the sink empty, but he would tell me I needed to dry out the sink. Why? Why can't I leave it wet? It's clean. Who is this hurting? I know some people were raised to dry out their sink, but it was my place and I ran it as I pleased. The list went on and on with him telling me how to run my household, how to clean according to his ways, just picking with me.

I always would rush home from work to make sure I was on time, or he would write me up that I missed my session. He knew what time I got off from work, but he would still schedule our appointment for me to have to leave work early to rush to pick up the kids from two different locations—daycare for my two-year-old and afterschool for my older two—to make it back to my apartment to his appointment on time. He really made my life a living hell, all because I couldn't afford the meds. I used to cry out to God, *"Please, please, please don't allow him to keep using his power over me."* Things were getting very uncomfortable because I wouldn't dare go up against him and he knew it. The sexual innuendos started, and I kept praying harder, praying that it didn't go too much farther than the innuendos. But I knew it was coming. Then one day he suddenly stopped coming, and I got a letter stating my case was closed. I didn't know why or what happened, but he definitely was using his power to intimidate me. Thank God my case was closed abruptly because I felt like the visits were going in a sexual direction for his benefit. I don't know what would've happened because I was scared he would use that to make bad reports and take my kids away if I didn't comply. I eventually did hear, but it wasn't confirmed, that the agency they were using with my caseworker was contracted out to DFCS. They stopped using them because something had happened. I really don't know the full story, but why do I need to? Thank you, God, once again, for intervening and answering my prayers right on time.

This just goes to show the things that happen when the agencies send out a male to be over a case with a single female or vice versa. I've had open cases where two people would come to my home on visits and cases where just one person came. Usually, when it's one, it's a female. This was a first for me that it was only a male, but that doesn't mean anything. A woman can abuse her authority just as much as any man. But that man was abusing his authority against me, preying on me as a single woman who would've done anything to keep my kids and he knew it. Everything he said up until that point, I did reluctantly. And he had fun watching me squirm as he preyed on his innocent victim. Just a little more time and he would've had me right where he wanted me. Without my prayers, this story could have gone differently, and all because I couldn't afford my child's medication as a struggling single parent. Yeah, it was my fault I forgot and accidentally let the Medicaid lapse. I tried to correct it and re-apply as soon as I found out it lapsed, but that just wasn't enough. This was just one of my many stories about the struggles of trying to raise my kids alone. Not having enough for necessities and almost being punished for doing the best I could by myself.

APARTMENT ROBBED

Do not repay anyone evil for evil. Be careful to do what is right in the eyes of everyone. If it is possible, as far as it depends on you, live at peace with everyone. Do not take revenge, my dear friends, but leave room for God's wrath, for it is written: "It is mine to avenge; I will repay," says the Lord.

Romans 12:17-19 (NIV)

While still in the Georgia projects, I was dating a guy. He had his own place and we both worked and had other responsibilities, so we didn't see each other as much as I had wanted. And the kids and I had a female puppy that my daughter named Katie. My little cousin, James, a 14-year-old, had been staying with me for a while before going back to stay with his grandmother, my aunt Debra. Unbeknownst to me, he befriended a kid in the projects. This boy popped up at our door one day and my oldest son, then 10 years old, opened the door. He asked me if I could make a plate for James' friend, who was at the door hungry. I went to the door and saw this

Apartment Robbed

extra tall, lanky boy, I mean at least six feet. I had never seen him before, so I asked, *"You're James' friend?"* He said they knew each other from the playground. I asked my son, *"You saw him before?"* My son said, *"Yeah."* I asked the guy how old he was, and he told me 14. Only 14? He was so tall. But ok. I asked him a couple of questions, then let him in to have a seat. He told me he lived in another building in the projects, up a few buildings from me. I asked about his mom. He said she was at work, so I told him he could stay and eat instead of sitting outside with the plate. While I was fixing the food, he went into the living room and played with my son on his Xbox. When I tell you the boy was hungry, he wasn't lying. He ate so fast, and I made him a second plate. This started a pattern of sorts. He would come over some days, eat, and play Xbox with my son after we came home from work and school. It didn't bother me because once I told him it was time to go, he left with no problem, and it wasn't an everyday thing.

One night, he showed up at my door. He needed a place to sleep. Why? Where was his mother? He said she was working overnight at her second job...Hmmm? So why wasn't he at his house sleeping while she was away at work? He said she didn't let him stay in the house overnight when she wasn't there. Hmmm? So I asked where he usually stayed overnight when she worked. He said anywhere, at different people's/friend's houses. I said I needed to confirm the bogus story. He called his mom from my phone and we talked. She confirmed he was not allowed in her house when she was not there. She didn't even sound sorry. She said she couldn't trust him alone in her house. I didn't get into the details, I just wanted to make sure his story was straight. I was thinking, *"She barely feeds him, and now to find out, he has to find somewhere to sleep some nights... AT FOURTEEN YEARS OLD???"* I thought surely it must be him just being a teenager, doing normal teen stuff to get him in trouble with his mom. Disclaimer: After having three of my own teens, I see things differently now. However, that was not his case at that time. I told him he could stay over for one night. It was on the weekend. He slept downstairs on the couch. It was that one and only time he slept there, but he did come over a few more times to eat and play Xbox with my son.

One day, I went home from work on my lunch break, a spur-of-the-moment thing. I walked into my apartment, which was reeking of a man's cologne. I wondered, *"Why did it smell so strong in my apartment?"* It stunk, like an old man's cologne. It must have been coming from outside, but I didn't smell it until I got into my apartment. I paid it no mind. I had no time to figure it out on my limited lunch break. I usually bought lunch close to my job at the TV station or took it from home. When I walked in through my back door, I thought I heard my front door close but when I looked, I saw it was shut and didn't bother to check the lock. Maybe I was hearing things. I would've gone straight to my kitchen to fix something to eat, but I noticed Katie wasn't barking. That dog always barks for someone to let her out of her cage, especially when she knows someone is in the apartment. I went to the living room to check on her. The doggie cage was open, and Katie wasn't in there. I always put her in there when we left the apartment. I yelled Katie's name all over the house while looking for her. I was mad at her because she was wasting the little bit of lunchtime I had left, thinking she found a way to get herself out. I went upstairs into my bedroom and stopped short. My room was ransacked, and the window was wide open. I panicked for a second but then looked for Katie again. She always came to me when I called. I thought someone stole her and left with her through the window, but then I looked under my bed and saw

Apartment Robbed

her. She was scared, not making a sound. After a few minutes of coaxing her slowly toward me, I saw her eyes bloodshot red. I finally got her in my arms and talked to her, trying to calm her down because she was shaking so hard. I didn't know what was going on with her but I assessed my room, looked at my open drawers, and realized I had been robbed.

I went through all the kid's bedrooms, and sure enough, we were robbed. I didn't get pissed off until I saw my daughter's room. Her drawer was also ransacked, but her panties were actually touched and thrown on the floor. I was livid! I felt so violated for my daughter. She was only 8 years old. It's one thing to go through my panty drawer, which they did, but my little girl's? I felt as if they molested her. She was so innocent. I was imagining them sniffing her panties. I assure you, my sons' underwear wasn't touched. I swore, whoever it was would pay for the mental and emotional damage they put me through thinking about my daughter. It didn't matter that they didn't physically touch her. As I said, when it came to my kids, I always defended them.

I went through all the rooms and assessed what was stolen. In my panty drawer, they barely touched them but just enough to push them over to get to my jewelry. All of my gold jewelry was taken except my name earrings and name chain. I wonder why? Perhaps they wouldn't be able to sell it to another "Keka." Really, no one else had my name, nowhere near that town. I went back downstairs, and yep, the Xbox and games were gone, my computer, and some other stuff I hadn't noticed when I walked in.

I called my boss, Mike, to tell him I'd be late returning from lunch. I called the police to file a report. While the police came to take the report, another man dusted for prints all over the house. What a mess I had to clean up. Both the ransacked apartment and the black powder dust everywhere. I found out my front door was unlocked, and there were at least three separate prints in the apartment. In putting everything together and talking with the cops, I concluded (my version of what I think happened, not the cops themselves saying this) that one person climbed up the side of my apartment building and went in through my side bedroom window that I never locked and then went downstairs to unlock the front door for the other two. Someone with a strong, pungent cologne was the lookout at the back door where I walked in, surprising them, and must've yelled to the other two. The one with the stinky cologne must've hauled a%# through the front door, which I heard close when I walked in, and the other two went back out through the upstairs window as they were both probably up there already anyway searching through the bedrooms. They didn't have time to close the window. Actually, why would they close the window? Thieves are not considerate. Scratch that thought. But Katie, I realized, must've been barking at them when they entered the apartment, so they took her out and beat her in her face to shut her up. When they let her loose, she ran to hide. Our poor Katie. More like my daughter's poor Katie. While the cops were still there, Mike stopped by to check on me. He ensured I was ok and told me not to worry about returning to work that day. Such a good guy he was to everyone around him.

 After that, I was scared to death to be alone with the kids in my apartment. Every night I thought, *"What if they come back? I don't have any weapons or any man living with me."* I made my kids sleep with me in my bed cuz if those thieves returned, I needed all of my kids together to defend them. Me with my butcher knife, under my pillow, and my son's metal baseball bat by the side of the bed, and ALL the lights stayed on. Either

Apartment Robbed

I would fight to defend them or we would all die together cuz I thought they were grown men with that stinky cologne smell. I didn't sleep well at all, especially the first few days. I literally feared for our lives every night. But one thing I know, I never showed my kids how vulnerable I was. It did break my heart to tell them about my son's Xbox and my daughter's Katie. My boyfriend took her to stay at his place with him until we could find her a home with someone else. I dared not leave her in my apartment alone anymore when we were out during the daytime for her safety, plus her anxiety and fear must've been higher than mine.

Time passed and I still fed the 14-year-old boy, who still came around. As soon as he ate, he left cuz there was no Xbox to play and he had nothing in common with my 10-year-old. I asked him a couple of times if he heard anything or knew anything about who robbed my place. He always said no. But that last time I specifically asked him if HE had anything to do with my apartment being robbed. He said no. I told him if I found out he had anything to do with that, after all that I did for him, he would be sorry. I would make sure of it. I told him I don't make light of my threats. I don't know what made me say that to him because I believed him, but the words still came up from my gut and out of my mouth.

I went back and forth with the police department, and they found nothing. They did not identify anyone from the prints. What a waste of my time. It just pissed me off more cuz they acted like it wasn't important enough. Meanwhile, I feared for my and my kids' lives every night. A few weeks passed and things started to die down, at least my fear did, and I started to feel safe again thinking the men weren't coming back. It was just my fear and imagination. What are the odds anyone would rob the same place twice? Robbers just move on to the next place. What else could they take if they had already robbed a place? After I set my mind to settle down, my apartment was robbed again.

This time, I walked in with my kids after a day of work. I picked them all up from their daycare and after school. I noticed the shift of atmosphere as soon as we went into the apartment, unlike the first time because now I was always on guard when I walked in. I walked around my place, and lo and behold...whatever they didn't get the first time, this time they cleaned me out. They took everything I didn't even know I had left. And how, just how did they walk out with TWO TVs??? My living room and bedroom TVs. Back then, these were no flat screens. They were big, clunky TVs. My neighbors had to see something. I cried silently, then became angry. I was pissed off! This was definitely an inside job. Whoever it was knew me and was watching me. They knew my schedule and knew I lived alone with my kids. They knew I never went home for lunch, so I surprised them the first time. They knew when the kids and I got home at night, so they had time to clean me out this time. Now, instead of being scared, I was pissed the f^&k off! God, tell me who it was so I can take care of it myself. I know ole boy said it wasn't him, but I just need confirmation to take care of it now! Whoever saw me as vulnerable, I was gonna show them I'm from the South Bronx, and they got the right one this time. I didn't even bother calling the cops. For what? So they can mess my apartment up again, taking more prints? I'm sure the same people who robbed me the first time had returned and apparently, the prints never helped them the last time. So if they couldn't find out who it was then, I would be on my own now. I would have to do my own investigation.

But I didn't even have to do an investigation. Didn't my God come through and give me my answer? And I didn't have

Apartment Robbed

to look far. Later that week, I went to the management office to pay my rent. The apartment manager, who always talked me to death, finally had something worth listening to. She talked to me as if I knew who robbed my apartment twice. And yep, it was ole boy, the 14-year-old teenager. She was going on about how she heard I had been feeding him and such, and wow! How could he do that to me? She has had problems with that boy and his twin brother since they moved in. She heard they started breaking into people's homes, people meaning mine, and she couldn't believe he, his brother, and their friends were being so bold robbing my place twice. On and on and on she went. She told me someone from the complex came to pay their rent and told her everything. WHOA!!! There I was oblivious to everything, well not really, my intuition told me. But I was feeling like the only fool because I went to work and back home with my kids and minded my business every day. I didn't have neighbors I spoke to but yes, word on the street was that everybody knew. Well, not everybody, cuz I sure didn't. Then I thought, *"IT WAS THAT SNEAKY A%# MF! I knew it! How dare he! How could he?"*

First I was hurt, but the longer I sat there listening quietly at her yacking away, the angrier I became. And WHAT?! A twin brother! I never... So was it him or his brother around me all those times I was feeding him? Would I have known the difference? Were they identical or fraternal? I didn't know and didn't ask. I had too much more on my mind trying to decipher. That no good a%# little boy. So either his brother, friends, or himself WERE the lookouts. But what bothered me was that I had neighbors who knew, and no one came to tell me anything. Instead, I was the talk of the town. Or did they think I already knew? Now I knew why his mother said he wasn't allowed in her apartment when she wasn't there. She knew her son. And if I think about it, it wasn't just the rule for him. It had to be for his twin brother too. Them two-no-good-having-kids. I should have gone by her words, even without the explanation she never gave, but it was too late. What could I do about all this was the question. By the end of the management woman telling me everything I needed to know, I was angry again trying to figure out my next move cuz he was not gonna get away with that at all. I paid my rent and left.

I was nice to that teenage boy, welcomed him into our home, fed him, gave him a place to sleep, had him around my kids playing with my son's Xbox, and he robbed us twice. That same Xbox that I worked so hard to get for my son with no money, but I wanted to make sure I got him something nice that he had wanted for so long that it was one or two years later after it came out before I finally gave in to get it for him. I made sacrifices to get that thing. We didn't even have cable because I opted to get him that gaming system. I was so proud, and he was so happy when I surprised him with it as a gift. I don't remember if it was his birthday or Christmas gift, but my son didn't have it anymore. It was short-lived.

Was that boy around both times just to scope out the place? I believe so because I had never let him up to the second landing with my or the kids' rooms. He always stayed downstairs but then again, the one bathroom was upstairs. I don't remember him ever using the bathroom, but I'm sure he did at some point because he was there eating plenty of times. What about the time he spent the night? He probably walked around upstairs while I was asleep. He also probably came back to eat some more, without playing the Xbox the second time, to feel me out and see if I knew anything about who it was after the first robbery, to see what I knew and see what was left for them to take. The second time, they took the rest of the Xbox games

Apartment Robbed

they didn't grab the first time along with other stuff, like my TVs. I remember thinking, *"Damn, so they just gonna take the games without the game system? Who does that?"* That's how I knew it was the same people.

My wheels were turning. I knew exactly what to do! I was gonna pay somebody to break his legs. Not kill him, but hurt him enough so he wouldn't go climbing into anybody else's windows. I didn't care if he was the one who climbed through the window to unlock my door or walked through the door. Either way, that's what I said when I called my boyfriend. Ahhhh, boyfriend wasn't feeling it when I went to him and asked him to find somebody or some bodies (plural) I could pay a thousand dollars to break ole boy's legs. I meant a grown man or men. He thought he was tough? I wanted to show him tough! And yes, $1,000. Back then, that was a lot of money in the hood. I definitely didn't have that kind of money back then. I couldn't even afford my daughter's medication, but you best believe I would've made that thousand dollars appear! I asked him because he was from Columbus. I knew he would know somebody who needed the money. We went back and forth about it. He kept telling me to let it go and just move on. Move on? Do they think they could get away with doing this to me twice? He asked what good it would do. It wouldn't solve anything. I wouldn't get the stuff back. I said it would make me feel better. I just wanted revenge!!! He didn't want to get involved with that mess because it would damage his career as a security guard for the gate at Fort Benning. I really started questioning his loyalty to me. Why wouldn't he want to make me, his girlfriend, feel better getting this boy back? Why was he being such a bi%*h about it? Those were the words that crossed my mind. I never said them out loud to him, but I kept calling him a punk a%# bi%*h, and I never looked at him the same again. Back in the Bronx, it would've definitely been handled. But there I was, feeling alone, as I always was. Me and my three kids. My boyfriend didn't even have my back. All he did was help Katie find a new home with his co-worker's family. But, I was younger back then. I really didn't understand the importance of keeping a good job, especially with a secured job contracted with the military. All I knew was that I was up in my feelings, and I wanted instant gratification.

I decided to leave it alone because I had no choice. I didn't know anyone who I could pay. But my cousin, who had stayed with me and befriended him, found out. I never said anything to him. I'm assuming my aunt or other cousins told him. One day, I came home to a surprise. James had whooped ole boy's a%# out in the complex. James was shorter but definitely had more weight on him, grew up in the streets of Virginia, and was tough like his father and grandfather. They took no mess whatsoever, and their loyalty was to their family. I never told him or faulted him, but he was pissed off. One day, I walked into my apartment and shortly after, heard banging at the door. I opened it and James came in looking crazy, huffing and puffing, blood on his white T-shirt. I asked, *"Hey, what's going on? Are you ok? Where is that blood coming from?"* He wasn't talking. Actually, he was standing there trying to catch his breath. Then more banging on my door. I opened the door and O looky looky… look what the cat brought in, ole boy who robbed me was at my door, begging me to tell my little cousin to give him back his shoe. I look down and notice the sneaker in James' hand. I was so worried about him being hurt and the blood that I didn't notice the sneaker. Then I look at ole boy with the one shoe on, a ripped shirt, and a bloody face. I don't know what happened before, but I can tell you James stepped up to the door, cursed him out, and told him to

Apartment Robbed

leave. He kept begging for his sneaker, and that was it. James snapped, pushed him away from the door, and there they went in the front yard fighting. James was beating his a%#. I want to say again although I didn't witness it the first time, the boy was screaming for mercy from James' blows. I was like, here's this tall, tough boy who ain't tough at all but crying for the beating to stop. I don't remember if I stopped the one-sided fight, more like a beating, because ole boy was bloody and had enough or if James let up on his own. I don't even remember if the boy ever got his shoe back. I know my oldest son was out there with me and some other neighbors watching the fight. Before we walked away, I yelled at him that he was lucky that was all he got cuz I wanted somebody to break his legs. I told him that because I wanted him to know how serious this was to me and how easily he got off. He probably didn't hear or pay me no mind, lying in the grass, but I felt good, knowing I told him what my plans had been for him and he just got lucky. I was so giddy and happy when I got James and my son back in the apartment. I was so proud of my little cousin. I never told him to do that, and I wanted that other boy to hurt worse. But that revenge was so sweet. It wasn't expected, but it was enough justice served for me. I was so relieved. I could finally sleep at night, not only because there was payback but not knowing who robbed my place and who may come back in the middle of the night had been terrifying. I vowed to myself that if it happened again, I was gonna make sure I found somebody the next time to break his or whoever's legs. But I never got the chance. Thank God that was the end of that.

It was quiet after that. About two months later, I went to pay my rent, and the manager lady was there talking away again. She told me he was locked up. The police had finally caught up to him about something else, and he had been in for a while. She wasn't exactly sure why he was locked up, but knew it wasn't about robbing my apartment. I was glad he was in there for something. Ain't no telling what else he was involved in, terrorizing other people. It's safe to say I never heard about him again from then until the day we left Columbus about two years later. I never knew what happened to that boy and his life or twin brother. And you know, me and boyfriend didn't last much longer after that.

ROOFIE

But the Lord is faithful; he will strengthen you and guard you from the evil one.

2 Thessalonians 3:3 (NLT)

You would think I would have had enough drug stories in my life or at least this book alone, but nah, my life was more complicated than that.

My good ole cousin Jenise. We had some wild times together. She was my Jaime in the latter years. Jenni and I were running the streets together. Back in North Carolina, she came to visit me many times before I started broadcasting school and my drug addiction. We slowed down tremendously when we both lived in Columbus, Georgia. We were getting older. I had just hit my 30s. I was still getting my party on whenever I could, but definitely not running the streets anymore like I used to. As broke as I was, I still always found a way to attend clubs. Nowhere near as often, but more than a few times. Even if I only had enough for the admission fee and bought one drink,

The Angels Are Watching

I was getting in to have a good time. Oh, and enough money to pay my babysitter for the night. Sometimes my aunt Debra or one of my other cousins, C.J., babysat my kids. They never asked for money but I did it out of courtesy. Especially because if they didn't watch my kids, I wouldn't be going anywhere. I wasn't exactly wildin' out like I used to. I couldn't hang in the streets every day of the week anymore and still get to work the next day. My body was deteriorating faster because of all the drugs and alcohol it had been through, and it was nowhere near over for my body yet. But I still had a little partying left in me.

One night we decided to go downtown to Club Oxygen on the Broadway strip. It was more what I called "the college kids' club" to the Columbus State University students. I was trying to keep up with the youngins, a mixture of Black and white people. We liked the versatile music and the vibe there, so we went that night.

We had been in Oxygen for a little bit, drinking and dancing together. Then Jenni danced with the dude she met, some Black guy. I finished my drink. A really young white college kid and his friend introduced themselves to me. The one guy offered to buy me a drink. I said yes, because it was free for me, and we walked away from my cousin and her dude and over to the bar. The one guy who acted interested told me to order as his friend walked away. I placed my order and turned around to watch the crowd as the bartender made my drink. My drink was ready, so I turned back around to pick it up and started sipping. After a few minutes, ole boy and I walked over to the dance floor. I saw my cousin still dancing with her dude. All I remember was me and ole boy dancing. Then it started to get foggy. I felt like I was dancing in slow motion. Then I woke up in a hospital bed in the Columbus Medical Center. I had blacked out.

Roofie

I looked up at the Black nurse standing over me with a nasty attitude, taking care of my IVs, and asked her, "What happened? Why am I here?" As nasty as she could muster, she told me I knew why I was there. I honestly and meekly told her I did not know why and asked if she could tell me. She said I knew exactly why I was there with all that cocaine in my system and that I did it to myself, so I should not act surprised as to why I was there. I was shocked. I first thought, "Damn, how rude she was." I told her I didn't do drugs. She told me more rudely not to lie to her. I had been doing cocaine, and it was all in my system. Right then my uncle David walked in, and she walked away from me. In my head, I was questioning if I had sniffed coke that night. I didn't remember and knew to stay away from it, especially after my history with it. I was scared to get hooked because it might lead me to other things again. But did I subconsciously use it while I was drunk? But I mainly remember, "Wow! This lady had no compassion for the sick." Then I told my uncle, Jenni's dad, what happened between the nurse and me, and that I really didn't know why I was there. He immediately told me I was drugged. I said, "What?" He told me someone slipped me a roofie, and some of them contain coke. He was matter-of-fact. No "must've been" drugged. He said I "was."

My uncle used to run the NYC streets before becoming a preacher. From the Red Hook Brooklyn projects, he knew what he was talking about. How he knew I was drugged, I didn't know at that moment. I later found out he got the story from my cousin before he walked in the back to see me. With his street smarts, he put two and two together. As shocked and mad as I was that I was drugged, I was so relieved to know I didn't do the drugs on my own accord. But when did the guy slip in the roofie? When I turned my back, waiting on the bartender to make the drink? Wow! Just that quick before I turned back around to grab it? And nobody saw him drop it in there? Or did they but didn't care? Minding their business? I felt ashamed, lying there in the hospital, thinking the nurse and staff thought I did it to myself and was a junkie once again. The shame. And once again, I couldn't shake that drugs still surrounded me wherever I went, even when I tried to stay away from them.

Jenni and I talked about that night around the time it happened. She told me she saw me falling all over the guy on the dance floor, and she pulled me away from him and got me to the hospital. But now as I write this story many years later, I hit my cousin up to ask her about leaving her car that night because I thought she had ridden in the ambulance with me.

Jenni's story:

> "Girl, I was the ambulance for you. That's what all the drama was about at the hospital. They didn't want to take you back because you weren't in an ambulance. I had to act an a%# and was almost arrested for them to bring you to the back.
>
> I did not have time to let you wait for an ambulance. I was speeding, running red lights and all. I had two guys—the Black guy and his friend—ride with me and help me carry you into the ER. The lady there was giving me a hard time, like she couldn't see what was going on, telling me I had to take you to a different entrance, and I spazzed out. I told her if she didn't open the f@#$ing door and take you back and something happened to you, I was going to f@*^ her up. That's probably why they called the police because I was not playing. Lol. The police came, dragged me out, threw

me on the hood of the car, and put handcuffs on me. The guys with me were both in the military officer's training at Fort Benning, so they were saying some sh!t to the police officer that actually got him to let me go. That night was crazy.

I had one of the guys that helped me with you call my dad. That's why he ended up coming up there.

The night of the incident, you were not just drunk. I knew that. Your eyes rolled to the back of your head. You couldn't stay awake. I had my guy keep shaking you and trying to get you to keep talking about anything to keep you from going to sleep. You were throwing up and saying you just wanted to sleep. I kept saying, *"Don't let her go to sleep."* That seemed like the longest ride to the hospital ever."

Ahhhh, now I understood the nurse's anger and attitude toward me after learning about the chaos that was created at the hospital because of me. And there I was thinking the nurse was mad at me because she thought I was doing drugs and ended up under her care, wasting her time. My poor cousin... my ride or die, straight from Brooklyn NYC, like her dad. She played no games! And when she made a threat, she held true to her word. So I thank God for her acting fast for me and things didn't escalate worse at the hospital. What would I have done if she did get arrested because of me? I don't know what that guy's plans were for me after I passed out, but he didn't plan on my ride or die to be there protecting me from him. It's all love to my cousin, my angel of the night.

FAMILY SPONSOR

Let your light shine before others, that they may see your good deeds and glorify your Father in heaven.

Matthew 5:16 (NIV)

This story is about how there are many charitable people in this world. I encountered them a few times as a single parent when help was offered to me by complete strangers. Here's one incident I'd like to share.

At the after-school program for my oldest two children, my family was chosen to receive a free Christmas tree. I entered the building as families were picking up their kids in the center's auditorium, unlike any other day because usually we picked up from their classrooms. In the auditorium, I was told to stand in front of everyone. The staff surprised me and told me my family was chosen by another family to sponsor us with a free Christmas tree. I had no clue. I didn't even know they did that. Apparently, they had a sign-up list, and a few families were chosen. I never signed up, but they chose me. I'm figuring the staff entered me. I even told them I never signed up. I was embarrassed standing there. No matter how hard life got, I never asked for handouts. Either I would make it happen or we would go without. Everyone was clapping for me after they announced it. Then they told me the donating family would be bringing the tree to my home. I felt very hesitant because I don't like to feel like a burden to anyone. I wasn't ashamed, I was just used to providing for my family myself, tree and all. I tried to tell them to give the tree to someone else because we already had one. We had a fake one, but hey it did the job. The kids didn't care whether it was real or not. What did they care about? The presents. So I told them we were good on the tree. But the staff wouldn't listen. Then I was told that with the tree came a lunch the next day. Myself and my kids had to attend the lunch with the family at a restaurant. I really tried to beg them to give away the tree and lunch. They would not budge. So I sincerely thanked them and took the information about the lunch.

Not long after I got home that same day with my kids, a white man came and brought the tree to our apartment. The same place where CPS had a case on me for my daughter's "neglect" of no medication, the same place we had been robbed previously. Like I said, we had some good times and some bad times living there. He asked where to set it up. I told him to just leave it at the door and I would fix it up. He was not having it. He set it up nicely in the living room and even dropped off bags of decorations (wow, they thought of everything), and told me he would see us all the next day. I truly thanked him and he left. The next day was a Friday. It was a late lunch, so I went to work and the kids went to school. I dressed them nicely but in regular clothes. I myself had on work attire. I told my boss Mike that morning, and he said it was ok for me to leave early.

The Angels Are Watching

I left to get my oldest two kids from school when it ended, instead of them going to the after-school program, picked up my third kid from the daycare, and drove us to the restaurant. We walked in, gave our name, and were taken to our table. Everyone sitting there was white. They stood up and welcomed us, hugged us, and introduced themselves. It was a long, big table of all adults. I didn't see any other kids. I wanted to die right there of embarrassment. I felt like a poor Black family getting "hand-outs" from white people for a show. I'm sure they meant well, as I recall them saying they did this every year. The after-school staff picked my family that year. I sat my children and myself down. I don't remember if I or my kids said their names to everyone. I don't remember what we ordered. All I remember was I wanted to cry. I had never felt so awkward and embarrassed. I don't remember any conversation or even if I spoke to anyone. I'm sure they asked general questions and I answered. I don't remember if my kids spoke. I don't even remember the conversations they were having amongst themselves and around me, but vaguely remember they were chatting, laughing, and having fun. My children and I were quiet the whole time. Once they started acting up, I gave them "that look" and they straightened up fast. All I remember was wanting to leave so badly. I also remember not ordering dessert when they offered it because I wanted to get out of there as fast as I could. At the end, when I thought I could finally escape, they announced they had presents for us. I nearly died. When I and the kids stood up to leave, a few of them told us they'd bring the presents to my car from their cars. I said my thank yous and goodbyes to the rest who stayed at the table, waiting for their desserts to arrive. I walked to my car and put the kids in. Bags and bags and more bags and boxes of wrapped gifts, big and small, were coming our way. I opened the trunk of my

Family Sponsor

jeep. I thought that was it, then they said there was more. They made a few more trips and even brought my youngest a bike. He was about three years old. They filled up my trunk, packed full. I said my thank yous and goodbyes again. They went back inside, and I drove off.

No pics were taken. Not in that era. There was no such thing. Anyway, I hope I didn't seem nonchalant and ungrateful. I just felt very awkward the whole time. When I got home, I unpacked the car and set the gifts under the tree that came with the brand-new decorations. They were definitely no rookies. They thought of everything. That day when I unpacked the car of gifts when the kids weren't around, I cried, thanking God. I didn't need to buy them a single thing that Christmas. The people had already put the kids' names on everything and distributed them evenly amongst all three. No one kid had more than the other, and everything was age and sex appropriate. Not just the toys, but even the sizes of the clothes. I did buy each one of my children a gift from me, just to say to myself I bought them something for Christmas, although I didn't need to. I was used to being the one to make sure they had a Christmas. We were all surprised when they opened their gifts on Christmas day the next week because I had no clue what was wrapped either. They had clothes from the Gap, Old Navy (that's when those names were a big deal,) and other brands, and toys, and were very happy. I even got a few things, like a bath set and shirts. They even thought of me. In the beginning, with the announcement, the tree, the lunch, the gifts, the whole process, I was so embarrassed. In the end, I cried and thanked God, and I was very grateful to Him and the family who gifted us. I didn't put in for the family donation, but I was grateful to God I was one of the few chosen that year. God knew my family needed it. I really thought Christmas wouldn't be like the kids were used to, with many gifts under the tree. I had to replace a lot of things that were stolen in my home. The one job at the TV station and the very little child support wasn't helping much because as we all know, I had children, bills, and daycare fees. I know that's life and everybody has bills just the same, but God always made way for my family. That year, my children had an awesome Christmas thanks to the lovely family that stepped up. I don't remember their names. They said they picked a family every year, so I know more families have been blessed by them. I hope they received their blessings right back. That year, our Christmas was provided for us by angels God sent to us in human form.

SISTERS WITH ANGELIC WINGS

Keep on loving one another as brothers and sisters. Do not forget to show hospitality to strangers, for by so doing some people have shown hospitality to angels without knowing it.

Hebrews 13:1-2 (NIV)

I want to share about two more women out of many who have blessed my children and me throughout our lives.

Months after the nice Christmas we were given, our joyful season ended. When it rains, it pours. First, my car got repossessed. I'll save the story about how that craziness went down. Just know it wasn't as simple as you'd think. There was a lot going on and police were called. But for those who live in New York City, the bus systems outside of New York are not so accessible. You have to go to a "hub" or "transfer center" to make transfers, which is only one designated spot for the whole city or selected places that are few and far between. There's no such thing as transfers from block to block, corner to corner. To get anywhere from place to place takes FOR-EVER! With

The Angels Are Watching

no car, I had to wake the kids up around 4 a.m. to get them dressed and fed and out the door to bus it everywhere, and I mean everywhere. First, we had to walk over a small bridge to the bus and ride it to my youngest's daycare, Kiddie Kollege, on St. Mary's Road, then bus it back to the METRA transfer center. We then transferred and bused to my oldest two's school. I would then walk the rest of the way to my job at the TV station because it was faster than going back to the hub and taking another bus. And yep, same steps backwards going home. That went on for a while. I cried almost every day because it was a bit much on the children and me. I especially cried because I felt their pain for them. They would be so tired in the mornings, they'd be sprawled out sleeping across the bus seats cuz no other passengers were on there so early.

One day the daycare owner, Ms. Juanita, happened to be there when we all dropped my youngest off. She was greeting everyone that morning. She was very involved with her business, and it showed. We got to talking, and that's how she found out about my situation. What did she do? Dropped everything, right then, and drove my kids and me to school and work. I tried to tell her not to worry about us, we were ok. But she wasn't having any of that. Every day, faithfully, when we showed up at the daycare, she would take us where we had to go, school and work. I told her I didn't have money to pay her, but she told me she wouldn't have taken it if I did have it to give. She was doing it out of the kindness of her heart, and she didn't mind helping us one bit. We were sooooo blessed to have met her. Good ole Ms. Juanita Lewis. She definitely went over and beyond when she didn't have to. I was so grateful for her. And thank God she didn't take "no" for an answer because she made our mornings so much easier, and our moods were much lighter. Truthfully, I now believe she was an angel sent to us. Had it not been for her, I'm sure another nervous breakdown would've been coming... and soon.

Simultaneously, I had become friends with the early morning bus driver. He would crack jokes so early in the morning... ugghhh, who wakes up that happy so early? We were on his bus route about 5:30-6 a.m. and occasionally, he would stop by my apartment to check to see if we needed anything because we had no car to get around. One time he picked me up from the supermarket instead of having me pay for the usual cab to get my groceries home.

He dropped by one early evening with the sun just going down. I opened my door and he stood inside my kitchen, as he normally did. He was usually there or in my living room for a few minutes whenever he dropped by just to say hi. He looked around and questioned my lit candles in the kitchen. I said, *"Oh, I just like candles. No reason."* Then he walked into my living room and saw more lit candles everywhere. He asked,*"Your lights are off?"* I said, *"No,"* confidently. He asked again. I said no again. *"I told you, I like candles."* He walked to flip on the switch, and I was busted. I was so embarrassed. That was the first time ever my lights were turned off and my car repossessed. I was batting a thousand, failing miserably at trying to keep my household together. Those bills were kicking my butt! A woman once told me if I ever had to figure out which bill I couldn't forgo, it was my rent bill. I would be able to make do with my family as long as we had a safe roof over our heads. So, there went the car and lights. He told me I couldn't live like that with my kids. It wasn't safe. He was going to find somewhere for us to stay until I got my lights back on. Always making it work for my kids and me and with my pride, I was like, *"I'm not going anywhere. We're staying right here, where we belong. We'll be ok."* He said ok and left.

The Angels Are Watching

Later that night, I got a knock on the door. A lady was standing at my door. She told me she was sent by my guy friend who worked with her at the METRA bus station. They also attended the same church, so she knew him well. She said she was taking us to her home. I politely declined, not because I didn't trust her. If my friend trusted her, I knew she was good. It was because of my pride and I didn't want to be a burden, especially on someone I didn't know. Once again, just like Ms. Juanita, I believe now that she was an angel Heaven sent because God's angels do not budge until they accomplish the mission He sent them on. So there was Ms. Loretta Stewart inside my door. She told me to gather some things for us and that she had extra bedrooms because her kids were all grown and lived in their own homes with their families. She assured me she had the space. We would not be a burden, and she'd bring us back to pick up some more things another day. After going back and forth, not knowing how to kick this nice woman out, I gave in so we could get on with our night. She won. She didn't take my no for an answer and most certainly did not leave without us. We were on our way to our temporary home that was much nicer than a shelter.

Ms. Loretta had three spare bedrooms. She told me we could utilize all the bedrooms so we wouldn't be crowded on top of each other. The first bedroom she showed us, I took. This room had a queen or king-sized bed, big enough for the four of us. I always wanted my kids with me. I always said, *"It's us against the world,"* and I meant every word. Just like all the shelters we lived in, we were in one room, although usually different beds. It was no problem to camp out in one bed. I needed eyes on them in one room and trust me when I tell you, we all fit in that bed and had extra space.

It just so happened I had filed my taxes and was waiting on my income tax check to come. I assured her as soon as it came, I would turn my lights back on, pay her kindly for her hospitality, and we'd be out of her hair again. Of course, she said no rush and no payment due. But nah! We gonna see about that.

Now regarding momma Loretta: She took to us so well and loved on us so hard, we became comfortable living with her those few weeks. After our long work and school days, we would all gather around in her kitchen for dinner and dessert or in the living room, watching movies on VHS tapes. We had many laughs and her home became a safe place for us. Instead of Ms. Juanita driving us every morning, Ms. Loretta took over before she started her day at work. What a gift from God to us. She did so much for us. Instead of my youngest going to daycare because I had to make some wise money adjustments, I started paying my aunt Debra to watch him again...a much cheaper rate. Again, she didn't want to take the money but I always gave her something as a thank you. Things were coming along nicely. During that time, momma Loretta would take me around on the weekends to look at cars and do some test drives so when that check finally came, I knew which one I was getting.

With a car that was used but new to me and the lights back on, it was time to move back to our place at Chase Apartments. Right before we left, momma Loretta's car started acting up, and she said she had to take it to the shop. Since she wouldn't take payment for us staying with her, I secretly gifted her the money for the repairs. I left the money in her car to find and told her to get her car fixed. So that was that! I won that battle with her, lol.

When we got back home, I started looking for a second job cuz your girl needed more money. I didn't want to be in that predicament again. I landed a position at WRBL News 3, aka a CBS-affiliated station. I want to say my boss, Mike, put in a word for me there because I know how he is, but he wouldn't admit it. I worked as a production assistant for the news department, then the media content manager/master control operator. In layman's terms, I was responsible for inserting all the CBS shows and commercials that were broadcast to viewers in a 24-hour period, except for when the live local news was on. When I tell you, ya girl made it! I was too proud of myself. I was working in television, doing more and more. Working at two TV stations, I had come a long way from almost not graduating due to my addiction in North Carolina. I was killing the game until...the sexual harassment started. I was so naïve to it in the beginning that once again, by the time I realized what was going on, I was so deep into it.

This was coming from a man of a high-ranking position at the station, who I will keep nameless, and who was well respected. I didn't dare go up against him. He was there way before me and would be way after me, although that's my assumption because I didn't keep track once I left. In the beginning, it wasn't so bad. I was able to nicely keep his advances at bay because I was clueless. His innuendos went right over my head from day one. Once I realized what was going on and I kept rejecting him, all hell broke loose. He was making it real hard for me to work there. I was constantly in the HR office having to show proof of my work being done proficiently and in a timely manner. Completion of my work was legit and so were my out-of-town meetings the company sent me on for training. My work ethic showed my capabilities every single time. I had no issues with my actual work but yet, I kept getting called into HR. If I hadn't provided the proof every single time, I'm sure I would've been terminated. There was actually an incident where I had to explain to HR my training at WKRG in Mobile, Alabama. I had to go into detail about the actual training, the trip to the location, my car issues, why I didn't work the designated hours in the designated time, the people I was with, the conversations that took place. I even went into detail to verify to them when I worked and how many hours I worked to make sure they understood I did what I was supposed to do. I was where I needed to be, and no funny business was taking place over the course of the training. I needed to give them every little detail to reassure them I was doing my job, and it was quite annoying at times. Here is a snapshot of the type of process I needed to go through to prove my innocence to HR, all because of one man.

October 8, 2008

To: Otis ▮▮▮

This letter is my documentation of my accounts of my training in Mobile, AL. at WKRG. Wednesday, October 1, 2008, I spoke with ▮▮▮, between 7 – 8am to let him know I would not be able to ride with him to Mobile, AL, as planned, because of personal reasons. On October 1, 2008 I left my house around 3:30pm to make my way to Mobile, AL. On the way there, I spoke to ▮▮▮, while on the Interstate to let him know I would be arriving later than planned. I arrived at the Motel 6 around 7:30pm. On the way to WKRG from the motel, I got lost and called ▮▮▮, to see if he would be able to give me directions other than what I had (which he could not help me). When I arrived at WKRG, around 8pm, I called ▮▮▮ again, to get the name and number of the person I needed to get in touch with while I was there. He gave me Raymond ▮▮▮'s name and I called Raymond on my cell and he came to get me at the front door. While I was in training, I called ▮▮▮ twice to get information on the names of the equipment we were using because the people training me (Raymond ▇▇▇ and Cynthia ▇▇▇▇▇) were asking information on what we used at WRBL. I finished my training around 12am. The next day, Thursday, October 2, 2008, I spoke with ▇▇▇▇▇▇ around 1:30pm and let him know I would be going back into WKRG for more training from 2pm – 6pm. I arrived at WKRG around 1:45pm and had been told ▇▇▇ had just left before I got there. I proceeded with my training and left around 5:45pm to head back home. In conclusion, I did 8 hrs. of training as planned.

*I will now explain what was planned, prior to the trip. ▇▇▇▇▇▇▇▇▇ and I decided to ride together to Mobile, AL, October 1, 2008. This was due to the fact my car was not running right and I had no extra money to rent a car. We were to meet at WRBL at 11am and leave from there. We were to arrive in Mobile, AL in time for me to be at WKRG at 4pm, to do training for 8 hrs. (4-12pm). The next morning, October 2, 2008, ▇▇▇▇▇▇ would be attending training in the morning and we would leave that afternoon, to come back to Columbus, GA. We discussed, **IF** I felt I needed more training, I would go back in on Thursday, October 2nd, at 4pm and stay only for a couple of hours because he didn't want to be driving back to Columbus, GA late at night. We discussed my hrs to train starting at 4pm because that was the shift the Media Content Manager was on duty, and that is my position I'm training as. On Thursday, October 2,2008, I decided to go back to WKRG to do some more training to make up my 8hrs., even though I didn't feel I needed additional training because their systems are set up differently from ours. What WKRG was training me on works only for their station. WRBL runs it differently* because our systems are not as updated as theirs. However, because I got in late Wednesday night, I took the initiative to make sure I did my 8 hrs., to comply with the reason of me going. Instead of me going in at 4pm, on Thursday, I was going in at 2pm. This was because one of the people training me there, was going in early at 2pm. So I decided to go in early to be able to leave early, to make it back to Columbus, GA. I got to WKRG, Thursday, around 1:45pm and left around 5:45pm. Together I did 8hrs of training as planned. I know I didn't do my 8 hrs in the 1 day planned, but because of personal reasons, I made it to Mobile, AL late and finished up with my training the following day.

This letter is written because of the speculation that I was not at WKRG for 8 hrs. Therefore, this is my documentation of my accounts for both days. I have attached

- receipts (with dates & times)
- cell phone records of placed and received calls
- Also, the names of people I trained with are as follows:
- Raymond ▇▇▇ (Wed. Oct 1st, 8pm–12am & Thurs. Oct. 2nd, 1:45pm–5:45pm)
- Cynthia ▇▇▇ (Wed. Oct 1st, 8pm–12am & Thurs. Oct. 2nd, 1:45pm–5:45pm)

Although the following people did not train me, I met with them and had a brief discussion about the training and equipment. I'm listing them because they are the Manager and Supervisor over the department I was training in. They are as follows:

- Francis ▮▮▮▮ (Thursday, October 2nd)
- David ▮▮▮▮ (Thursday, October 2nd)

I would also like it to go on record that I did meet with ▮▮▮▮ *Monday, October 6, 2008 and we discussed the whole trip ordeal and what I did learn from the training. Also note that I did verbally apologize to* ▮▮▮▮ *for not giving him a courtesy call letting him know ahead of time that I was going to be late, instead of waiting until I was on the road. I told him, I should have called him earlier.*

I felt the need to write this letter because I value my job and my position. I wanted to clear up, that my intentions were to go according as planned. However, due to an unfortunate situation, things changed on my end. I do apologize for splitting my shift. I also would like to say, if ever given the chance again, it would be done differently. Again, my job is very important to me and I would like to have longevity with WRBL and continue being the hard worker I am, and to grow with the company, as a valuable employee.

Thank you for your time,

Nayo Samuels (Keka)

Cc: HR File

That is my original letter I saved on my desktop after all these years. It serves as an example of the many ways I had to provide proof to HR and the station manager to clear my name of any wrongdoing to keep my job. I was originally hired and started out in the newsroom production department but after a while, I applied for another position of media content manager. I had to go to another station in another state to do extra training. When I got back, I was called into HR and was told not only did I not show up there, but I had been seen in the Columbus, Georgia, downtown area the night I was supposed to be training in another state. All the lies. The HR rep had suggested I write the letter to the station manager explaining my side of the story. That was the many of firsts before she caught on to the shenanigans.

That went on for months until the HR rep realized something and started asking me questions. She could not understand why this man was going so hard against me with all the accusations because I showed her my evidence every time. She noticed he was making things up. She asked me, without asking me, if he was harassing me. I figured that approach was because she couldn't put the words in my mouth, so she was trying to get me to tell her. I told her without telling her, and we understood each other. I never came out and acknowledged her assumptions with a yes. After a couple more times in her office, she started to become upset with me. She told me she could only file if I made a complaint. I don't know why she was pressuring me so hard. She was a lovely white woman, but she was really upset because I wouldn't budge on my story. I assumed she really wanted to help me or to protect the station, as the latter was her job. But again I "verbally" told her, I wasn't being harassed and I didn't want to file a complaint. When she asked me why not, I straight up told her I wasn't trying to get anyone fired. I was not in the business of taking money out of anyone's pockets. He had a family of his own he had to provide for. I told her I could handle it. She was so mad and tried to convince me one last time. I left her office and did not see her again. She went on maternity leave and whoever temporarily replaced her never called me back into the HR office.

Many incidents later, after she had gone on maternity leave, the sexual harassment changed into just plain ole nasty harassment. Some next-level sh!t. It got to the point where I started to be unhappy with work. The field where I worked so hard to get into and was so proud of in the beginning was making me feel drained every day at the station. In the beginning, he was going behind my back to get me fired because I didn't have sex with him, but it turned into just plain ole bitter harassment in my face. I guess he knew if I was gonna snitch on him, I would have done so already. He knew he was free to treat me anyway he wanted because I wasn't telling HR anything. I was ok during my morning tv job but once I went there for my evening shift, I dreaded it. It took so much out of me just to walk into the station. I never told anyone. It was so hard. Altogether, I lasted there about two years but it became so unbearable that I decided to leave not just the station but Georgia. Ultimately, he took my joy of working in the broadcasting field. I could have just left there and stayed at the other station, but I was broken mentally and emotionally. It also took a toll on my body physically. I was so drained, like I didn't have life left in me. I had to escape everything. I asked myself, *"What was the point in staying if my joy of what I loved was taken from me?"* So I put in my two-week resignation and left Georgia on a whim. As soon as my two weeks were up, we were gone.

Before I put in my resignation, I tried to transfer my job to the CBS station in New York, but it was taking too long. I just wanted out. I told myself I would figure things out when I got back to New York. It didn't take me long to pack us up and, once again, move back up to New York City. When everyone asked me why we were leaving, I told everybody a different story but never the truth because I was embarrassed. My mood and how well they knew me influenced the story they got. Before I left, I accomplished my goals and dreams of working as a producer on some shows at CCG-TV. I was exceptionally proud of myself for having worked at two TV stations. Remember, I had wanted to work behind the scenes in the broadcasting industry way back before I even had children. Working in the entertainment field had been a dream embedded in me since I was a little girl. My mom can vouch for that, with all the extracurricular acting and modeling activities both my parents put me in as a young girl, before I started acting up and acting out in them streets. I started out wanting to be in front of the screen, but eventually my desire was to be behind the scenes, and I did just that! After working so hard to get into the career I wanted for so long, I was too embarrassed to let anyone know that I had let someone run me away from my dream. But those were the days when I was young and weak-minded.

Goodbye CCG-TV, WRBL, and Columbus, Georgia.

Once I got back to my old self, I promised myself that if I was ever sexually harassed or had any kind of harassment again, I was gonna handle it differently. I wouldn't let it go so far as to break me down again. I would definitely not lose that battle again. Lesson learned. And all because I didn't want to get someone fired or made a fool of because of his status within the company, I had tolerated it way too long, until it was too late. I was looking out for someone else above my own needs. Gone are those days when I would let any person run me out of anywhere ever again.

16
JOINED THE ARMY

He giveth power to the faint; and to them that have no might he increaseth strength.

Isaiah 40:29 (KJV)

We were back in the Bronx living with my mom in 2010. I was looking for a job because with all the competitiveness within the broadcasting industry, especially in the heart of Manhattan, there was no way I could just jump right into any station without a transfer, not even the CBS affiliates. It was gonna be a while. I applied everywhere, and I mean everywhere. McDonald's didn't even hire me. Back on welfare and with my less than $100 a month of child support, I was barely putting gas in my jeep and providing for my kids. So what did I do? Join the Army Reserves at the age of 34 with three children.

This story is told to answer one of two questions about my life that I'm usually asked. One is why did I join the Army so late in life? There you have it, to have a steady income! My thoughts were to do what I had to do to provide for my kids. I needed money! I didn't want to join active duty because I was tired of moving my kids around. I wanted to give them a little bit of stability for once. The one weekend a month reserves' money with the welfare and child support money would help me until I could find a full-time job anywhere. I promise I was looking everywhere. Eventually, after basic training, I landed work as a housekeeper in the hotels through a temp agency.

Before I got there, I became a soldier first, but they didn't just let me in. Remember that domestic violence arrest back in North Carolina? That came back to haunt me, even though I had forgotten all about it. But they do an intensive federal background check, so my process to get in was a little more than your average person. I had to get a disposition from the court, and good luck with that whole process. It was just a big ole mess when you can't just walk into the courthouse to request your records. I was doing it from out of state and got the runaround for months. Then I had to re-do a whole investigation within the Army based on my account of what happened. My testimony of self-defense made them accept me, but I had to get a waiver to get in. So I almost didn't make it into the Army because of that arrest and because I was near the cut-off age limit. Whew! I barely made it in.

Once in basic training, the struggle was real. WHO???!!!... I mean WHO told me to join the Army with no athletic training EVER!!!!???!!!! We can't count the fighting all my younger life, although I wish that had trained me better. Those young kids coming straight out of high school were physically fit by default because of their age. Uggghhh! And especially the ones who were on sports teams in high school, the real athletes. Don't get me wrong, they all struggled too, but let's not compare our struggles, ok? A 34-year-old with lack of muscle control and elasticity due to body changes from giving natural birth to

The Angels Are Watching

THREE children and all the drugs and alcohol running through my body's system all those years. But there I was, keeping up and doing the thing! I was determined! I always accomplished my training in time but as I would come running in later than most, my platoon nicknamed me "grandma." They were on the sidelines motivating me to finish: *"C'mon grandma. You can do it! Almost there!"* Oh, and let's be clear, our Guidon Bearer who nicknamed me grandma did it to make fun of me. He was so annoyed with me the whole time we trained because I was an "old lady" in his platoon. My age was never held against us because we still won competitions against other platoons in our company. I had not slowed us down, so I really don't know what his problem was. I just think he thought I was too old to join, or felt like I wasn't fit enough to his standards or strong enough to be a soldier. But so be it. I had a family to feed back home while he had mommy and daddy still taking care of him, and I lasted longer than some of the other soldiers there. It never bothered me because I was only there for one thing, an income for my kids. After the name caught on from him, the rest of them were saying it out of love. We helped to motivate each other through basic training. Through it all, I caught bronchitis and sprained both ankles. First the left, then when that healed, the right. It was never-ending. But I trained through it all and graduated. Let's just say, everyone doesn't make it through basic training. Some recruits are "recycled" and may have to re-do training over from the beginning, which means they have to stay longer to finish, if at all. But like I said, I was determined because of my kids. I refused to be recycled. All I wanted was to make it back home to them. I missed my little hearts so much during that time, so much that one of my drill sergeants took to me. It wasn't said out loud, but he cared enough to make sure I made it through to the end.

Joined The Army

One day, we were eating in the chow hall. Soldiers were not allowed to look at one another. Straight ahead or head down. No eye contact or anything. I bent my head over my food and the tears silently started rolling down my face. I had my head down so no one would see. I was sitting there eating and missing my kids. I couldn't get home fast enough, so the tears came. This drill sergeant saw me, walked over to me with my head down without knowing why I was crying, whispered to wipe my tears immediately before any other drill sergeant saw me and came over to chew me out, then walked away as fast as he walked over. Yea, they're there to make your life hell. Ok, I'm kidding. But while they were doing exactly that, the intention was to break you mentally and physically and train you back up to the Army standard. He hushed me so the others wouldn't make an example out of me in front of the entire chow hall full of soldiers from the different companies. I remember back at our barracks, aka the "bays," some of the females asked me what he said to me to make me cry? That's what it seemed like. I told them I was already crying when he walked over and basically told me to shut up before I got myself in trouble, lol. They had only looked at me when he came to me because remember, we couldn't look at each other while eating. Nobody knew I was already crying. He spotted me before anyone else could. Thank God because things would've really gotten ugly if any other drill sergeant saw me.

Remember I had the two sprained ankles those few months of training? I promise you, I was probably walking without a limp the first two to three weeks of being there. After that, I was limping walking, limping marching, limping running, limping climbing—you get it, limping all throughout the training. So guess what? I had another nickname. A different drill sergeant named me McLimpy. Why the Mc in front? I have no clue. He was yelling at me throughout the whole basic training, calling me McLimpy instead of my name, and then I had the soldiers calling me grandma. Did anyone even know my real name? That's a joke. Of course they did. If we passed all of the Army training, at the end we got to take the physical training test one last time before graduation. If we failed, no graduation. Good luck to us all, especially me with my running limp. I still had to make my run on time before the clock ran out.

If I was running behind before for whatever the reason, that last day I was way behind. So behind, I started to give up. Of all days, all of a sudden, I had so much pain in my ankle and no motivation. I had taken ibuprofen that morning. I was like, "F^&k it!" Last day and I said I couldn't do it no more. I started walking because I was done running, which puts you behind time even more. Out of nowhere, that same drill sergeant who came to me in the chow hall ran up to me and screamed at me to get my a%# moving. And I mean, he didn't come to play nice. After he got me to start running again, he ran the whole way back with me while motivating me and singing cadence, up until about the last quarter of the mile, then he ran off and left me. If it wasn't for him, I wouldn't have made it to the finish line. I still made it before a lot of the younger kids, with my limp and all. I was proud of myself, like I was really doing something not coming in last. But I don't know why he chose to bless me both those times. I would hope that he understood I was really making an effort through all my illnesses and pain to get through to the end and not give up as others did along the way. My willpower was strong just some days, we all need reminders and encouragement to keep moving forward. I hope to think that's what he saw in me and why he chose to help me. I'm not sure if he helped others like that in his drill sergeant career, but he was definitely an angel sent to me. Do I think

Joined The Army

I would've graduated without him that day? Good question. I don't care to know the answer.

Again, I didn't want to attend my graduation but unlike my previous graduations, I had no choice in the matter because I was still signed over to the U.S. Army, aka Uncle Sam, and was forced to participate. I didn't invite my family to attend, even though other families were there. I didn't want the fuss or attention and just wanted to get home. Of course, when my mom found out they all could've gone to witness my graduation, she was upset. But no money was spent flying everybody out for a couple of hours to be with me. Instead, I went home a soldier and was able to spend all the time we needed together with the money I would've used to fly her and my children out and pay for lodging, food, and local transportation. Money was saved to take care of my family back home, as this was my only income. Mission accomplished.

Although I joined to provide for my family, the Army became such an amazing experience for me. I matured and gained so much knowledge. It was definitely different and more disciplined than me running the streets. It toned my behavior down a lot. I didn't have to renew my contract over the years, but I did. I accepted and recited the oath every time. And while it was successful in holding me down in the beginning until I found full-time employment—first as a hotel housekeeper, to CNA, to PCT, to being an LPN (nurse)--the end result was that I trained to fight and defend my country. That will always be the priority of the Army and the intent behind why I signed the dotted line every single time over any of my personal reasons. If they had to send me away in a war, guess what? It would be the risk of sacrifice I would have to take, knowing I may never make it back to my kids and family. But what was the bigger picture? Either way my kids would be taken care of and that was my intent by any means necessary. I had to do what I had to do being a single parent with no income and very little child support. I had to do any responsible thing I deemed fit.

But the Army was also a good ride for me. The long-standing benefits opened many doors and opportunities for me and my children. Family health insurance, kids' college funds, paying for my nursing school degree, soon my ministry degree, and all of the other perks. I'm not mad to have chosen this. While it is hard on lots of us soldiers and our families during the away trainings, wars, and deployments whether peaceful or not, I wouldn't change the fact that I joined. I still have a few more years left before I can retire and get my full pension. Over the years, with all the training I continue to get, I have gotten stronger and more physically and mentally fit. That was a plus I gained. That, and if I had not made it in, I would never have met my husband in the Army and had my fourth child. So no love lost there for me. The Army has been really good overall for me, my children, and our growing family. I gave of myself to the Army and in return, they gave back to me and my family.

17
UPSTATE ARREST

Yea, though I walk through the valley of the shadow of death, I will fear no evil: for thou art with me; thy rod and thy staff they comfort me.

Psalm 23:4 (KJV)

Every year, our families get together to enjoy and celebrate in all the festivities. The annual family reunion in 2012, however, proved to be different.

That year the reunion was in Ellenville, New York. Some of us decided to go to the club to end the night. We were at one of my cousin's houses making this decision. One female in the mix, Rosie, was a neighbor of my cousin. It was my first time meeting her. So we were all like, cool, the more to come with us, the merrier. I don't remember the name of the club, but we had a few cars full and drove to the club over in another county, Wurtsboro Hills, New York. Rosie knew the way, so she led driving my car. Ever since that near DUI in 1997, I never drove again when drinking, but I didn't mind getting in the car with others who drove drunk.

The Angels Are Watching

We got there fine and partied but on the way out, Rosie and I got into a heated argument about who knows what. I don't remember. We were drunk. We headed back with the three cars. My car, not the lead car anymore, was in the middle with the same driver, Rosie. I was sitting in the back seat behind Rosie. An argument started between my cousin next to me in the back seat and her boyfriend in the front passenger seat. Amongst all the chaos of yelling, cursing, and screaming between the two, my cousin pushed her way to the front seat and started fighting with her boyfriend. Fists were being thrown back and forth. I don't know if Rosie was hit or knocked into by accident or was just tired of us—the whole ordeal with her and my argument earlier and the fighting in the car or just us being a drunken mess—or she was just drunk and discombobulated herself. But she started speeding, driving erratically, and swerving around the side of the mountain, per the words of the people in the car behind us. All I remember was feeling like I was bouncing up and down in the car. Never-ending bouncing. I just thought we were driving on a really bumpy road. I couldn't see anything. Upstate in the mountains in the middle of the night, it was dark. You had to live there to know your way. That's why she was our driver. There's no streetlights like in the city. So it was just bouncing, darkness, and then stillness. Then there was yelling and my sister and cousins, from the car behind us, were pulling us all out of the car. They walked us up and sat us down on the ground, lined up along the side of the road. Everyone was talking and yelling and I wasn't understanding a thing being said. The car ahead of us was long gone and didn't know we had stopped. I had no idea what was going on.

Once I was able to understand, I realized we were in a bad accident. It was a crash with my car over the rail down on the mountain cliff. I didn't know how bad at the time. The occupants in the third car following us came around the curve, saw the accident, and got out to help us. Then Rosie went back and forth talking about how she couldn't go to jail because they would take her son away. I was trying to talk to her and piece together what she was rambling about but with everyone around talking, I barely could understand what was happening myself. She told me she had a CPS case opened on her and she was out past the curfew they set for her. They would take her son for neglect. He was at her place with her father watching him so she could hang out with us that night. Now I assure you, I didn't know the girl but I knew a thing or two about CPS trying to take your kids away. I didn't know her story but the fact she said neglect and not abuse, I understood. I mean, they said I neglected my daughter because I couldn't afford her medications in time. So did Rosie really have a case for neglect or what they assumed was neglect? Either way, my heart went out to her. I told her no worries, if asked, I would say I was the driver. The last thing I wanted was somebody's kid getting taken because we all agreed to go out partying. My cousin, one who was in the third car, said he'd take the rap because he wasn't drinking that night so he wouldn't get in trouble. So we agreed that night that he would take the rap for Rosie. I don't remember who called my Uncle Wade or about the ride back to his house, but we left my car in the ditch and everyone who was riding in my car was in my uncle's car going back.

I woke up a few hours later with the sun up. I couldn't feel my left arm. It was numb. My mom took me to the Ellenville Regional Hospital and I found out I had a fractured shoulder. While in the room, the police came to arrest me. Why? Because I left my car at the scene of the accident. That and they wanted to charge me with a DUI. No one thought to call the police about the accident, at least I didn't. I was never in an accident before so I didn't know I had to call. I thought I would just take care of my car being removed from the ditch for insurance purposes to see if it had to be totaled or whatever they did. I just wanted my insurance money to get another car. That's not how it works, but what did I know? It was my first accident. Apparently they found me by my registration papers in the car with my name and that led them to the hospital. My mom was there, telling me to tell the officer I wasn't the driver. But I couldn't tell him that. I didn't want them to take Rosie's son away. So I didn't say I was the driver, but I didn't say I wasn't the driver. They arrested me for leaving the scene of an accident. I figured I would get with my cousin later and he would take the rap for Rosie.

My cousin was really trying to help out with the situation and I know he meant well, but with all the back and forth to court with re-adjourning and re-adjourning and re-adjourning my case, I just told him I would take the rap for it because it was taking too much of his time for him to come from out of town. Both of us were from out of town, but he lived even further away than me and we had to go back every month. This went on for months. Finally, I convinced him to not worry about me with the case.

When it was all said and done, I had to do DUI classes that I paid for and I paid to reinstate my license after my classes were done. That and the court fees. Damn. I took the rap for Rosie but not only did it cost me my time but a lot of money, too. And I never heard from the girl again, not even a thank you or nothing. My cousins told me she couldn't be found after that night. They didn't see her again until a few years later but at the time of the accident, they couldn't find her. She had left her apartment. I assumed she thought I wouldn't keep my word and would rat her out, but I didn't. I kept my word, just like I didn't rat on ole boy with HR. There I was again looking out for others who didn't give a rat's butt about me. On top of taking the rap, boy o boy, all the wrath I got from everybody else around me who found out I didn't even know the girl. They told me I was a total fool. They didn't say it to my face, but I'm sure they all wanted to. I wouldn't even recognize her if I saw her again because I was drunk the one and only time I saw her. Ahhhh... but again, that was my decision that I made, and I stuck with it.

My uncle took me back to retrieve my things from my totaled car at the shop, then took me to the scene of the accident. I realized my car was less than one inch away from the bank that dropped OFF the side of the mountain cliff. This story was to tell you how God had His angels ONCE AGAIN surround me and my family in that car. Everyone who went to see the spot was in so much awe that we were so close to the edge and made it home alive. I was the only one hurt and thank God it was just my shoulder. All that bouncing I felt was the car rolling over and over and over down the side of the mountain. My car was completely totaled. It was only by God's grace and mercy that all of us in the car are still here and I'm alive to tell this story. Amen.

NYPD RAID

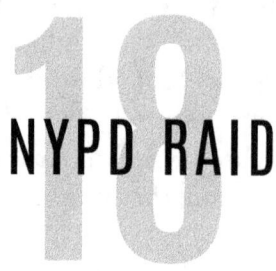

Though a host should encamp against me, my heart shall not fear: though war should rise against me, in this will I be confident.

Psalm 27:3 (KJV)

Initially, this story was just going to be about the details of the NYPD raid and the wrongdoings of police officers on my family in my mom's apartment in 2013 when I was still living there after leaving Georgia, joining the Army, and my DUI. However, I have a more pressing matter that was going on simultaneously that I want to address about the corruption of the NYPD.

But first, the raid. Police had the wrong apartment. I told them that from the time they banged on the door in the early morning and asked by name for a specific person who did not live in our apartment. I told them numerous times that I didn't know the person by name or the picture they showed me. The fact that I even asked for a warrant for them to enter, they never showed me, but just bum rushed into our apartment, knocking my pregnant self back with my fourth child. I'm assuming they thought I was lying to them so they were gonna "show me." Believe me, it was an ugly scene with all the commotion with shields, vests, guns drawn, flashlights blinding us, many officers running rampant and searching throughout our small, cramped apartment. Early in the morning meant more like in the middle of the night when everyone in the household was barely awake and still trying to figure out what was going on. All they needed, or not, was one wrong move. And all my kids were there and witnessed everything. I would hate to even think about what could have happened. The fact that as a U.S. soldier I couldn't do anything about it was disgusting, especially when the myth is told that all federal government employees take care of each other. They didn't have a warrant and we told them they didn't have the right to enter, yet they still rushed our home. This happens in the Black communities all the time. And I hate (strong word) when people say, know your rights, if the police don't have a warrant, don't let them in... I think that only works in the white communities...

Anyway, this was way before the murder of Breonna Taylor (RIP), however, when we in the community spoke up against it before, it fell on deaf ears. Why? Because cameras and video recordings weren't around then to hold law enforcement accountable. But just know, all those including young children (as mine were) and babies involved who have to witness these things can experience life-long trauma. And for those naïve and ignorant people who say law enforcement must've had a right to enter, "they" must've done something wrong for them to approach our home. NO! We did not! That's why we won a settlement against the NYPD for their negligence. But what is money from law enforcement settlements when they murder someone's loved ones? Especially, the "wrong" someone? And for my situation, what is money if your small children have nightmares after witnessing negligence and/or wrong-doing? I do know not all cops are corrupt, but if the shoe fits... Even though the system is against us, there are some good ones out there. Some I personally know, like my own family members or my fellow Army comrades who are in law enforcement. But thank God now for new technologies so the world can see what's really going on in the Black and Spanish communities.

What about the corruption of the NYPD? I started to witness it a few years earlier when my oldest was 14, just a teen during the "Stop and Frisk" era. I asked his permission to speak on this and some of what he encountered without much detail of his stories. Why am I making this my story in my memoir? Because of the frustrations and grief I experienced as his mother. The frustration of not being able to assist my helpless and hopeless son. So yes, this is still my story too, as I was indirectly involved.

I still don't understand why the NYPD decided to implement bogus arrests on our young Black and Spanish boys during that specific time because the "Stop and Frisk" law was passed in 1968 by the Supreme Court. Actually, I do understand. It was to finally make their quotas and to kill our young boys mentally and spiritually. Both were damaged further through the racism police had against our communities. I Googled the real reason for "Stop and Frisk." It was initiated for "reasonable suspicion that a crime had been committed." Then, and only then, should police stop and frisk a person, which may or may not lead to an arrest. But BAY-BAY! When I tell you how corrupt they are! They were arresting my teen son and his friends for absolutely no reasons, most times making stuff up. Let me run down a few of the absurd reasons they gave for arresting my son after numerous illegal "Stop and Frisk" incidents.

NYPD Raid

The very first arrest was for carrying a black sharpie in his book bag. Coming off the Grand Concourse New York City bus from high school, he was walking home and was stopped and frisked. Charge: "Gang Paraphernalia" This sincerely broke my heart because not only was it a bogus arrest, but I had bought him his school supplies that he carried to school every day. I was very confused when I had to go pick up my minor from the precinct and they told me that he "could have" used it for gang paraphernalia. What?!? For a potential crime, something that he never committed? My heart was broken for him. His first arrest at 14 for something he did not do. And then it just kept going from there.

- Arrested in McDonald's for sitting and eating for more than 30 minutes. Stopped and frisked. Charge: "Loitering"
- Arrested outside and in front of his own building while hanging out and talking with friends. Stopped and frisked. Charge: "No ID"
- Arrested in a friend's building lobby when walking to his friend's apartment. Stopped and frisked. Charge: "Trespassing" in a building that he didn't live in, although he was walking to visit his friend.
- Arrested at a house party for a different friend's birthday. Actually, a lot of kids were arrested that night. Stopped and frisked. Charge: "Trespassing" in the apartment of a friend who invited everyone in. They all won that lawsuit against the NYPD but again, what's money if it still goes on their record?
- Arrested for sitting on public steps, chillin with friends, by 170 Street, Grand Concourse, close to the public shopping area. Those who live in

the Bronx know there are steps everywhere in the neighborhoods. Stopped and frisked. We forgot what the charge was for, but they were picked up for what I felt was a made-up situation about my son and his friends chasing someone with bats. There were no bats found or any weapon on them when searched. No one came forward to say they were being chased. End result: Still got arrested for it.

- Arrested for playing basketball in the schoolyard. They stopped his game to search him and the guys for no reason. They were just driving by the yard and as usual, saw some little Black boys and decided to stop and frisk them. Charge: "Illegal weapon." My son was carrying my Army Gerber knife on him and they arrested him in the middle of his game. When I did the research on it, of course the pocket knife was under the size that was legal to carry, but nevertheless.

- When my son was about 16 years old, he had to go to trial after one of his bogus arrests for an officer's lies about my son assaulting him. Apparently, after another stop and frisk, he was in the precinct handcuffed to a bench. Words were exchanged because he was, again, illegally arrested. The officer choked him while my son was in cuffs. When my son yelled he would sue them for choking him, the officer got scared and concocted a story that my son grabbed his wrist and twisted it, and that was why the officer choked him. They took my son to trial for assault on an officer when actually, the police assaulted him. At the trial, the white cop had fake medical documents from his doctor saying his wrist

NYPD Raid

was fractured. He also had a Spanish female officer give her story that she witnessed my son attacking her fellow officer. My son later told us that he never saw that female officer. It was only male officers there that night. At any rate, we know they all cover for each other. Even the doctors cover for them with fake documents. My son's white, female, appointed legal aide was no good. Every court date, my mom and I kept telling her what to say and ask when she did her questioning because she was not, absolutely not, asking ANY of the right questions that would prove the officers' lies. She was timid and never did what we asked of her. She got run over by the prosecutors. Either she was new or didn't want to help a Black boy's case against the police for her own sake and reputation. My son never got the chance to testify because after all the cops testified and days with much of the back and forth at the trial, the white, male judge started asking his own questions. First, he found out the female officer wasn't present that night. Yay! Finally, someone was asking the right questions. His question to the female officer was how could she have witnessed anything if she wasn't there? The judge continued asking questions and realized their whole timeline of accounts was off. Then the judge asked the male officer to show how my son was cuffed. After his demonstration, the judge asked how could my son be handcuffed to a bench with his hands BEHIND his back AND still grab and assault the officer to inflict a fracture? I and my mom were like, *"YES!!!! Finally!"* The judge saw this was all a lie against my son. My mom was in the courtroom bawling. I knew they were happy, relieved tears running down her face. I sat there trying to hold it all together. What a relief! Those cops stop at nothing! The judge dismissed the case. I was very shocked at the dismissal because I just could not believe an old white man would be fair and call the liars out. I really felt like they all stuck together against our Black community, but that day proved me wrong.

I still had to go through hell and back during the "Stop and Frisk" era. All the times my son was arrested, my mom and I took turns picking him up from the precinct. Whichever one of us wasn't at work. It became a game for the cops. They knew my son and his friends so well, they were calling them by their family nicknames every time they stopped them. Stopped asking for IDs. They just made up stories to arrest them. I remember one day sending my son to the store down the block on Mt Eden Avenue and he never made it back home. This was really a game to the police. I know they would say they were just doing their job because they were forced to do the bogus stop and frisks, but they were doing them ONLY in certain communities. There was pure hatred and discrimination against our young boys. Our boys never had a chance, and the cops were enjoying it too much. I was told they always laughed while they were arresting our boys. It didn't matter if we moved. It was happening all over New York City in the underserved communities, so moving would not have solved the problem. And don't you dare say to keep our boys cooped up in the house. Really? So catch a case with CPS because our boys would then not be going to school? They were being arrested going to and from school. There was

NYPD Raid

no way out. The only solution was for the law enforcement to stop the madness.

Let me explain the real problem this "Stop and Frisk" era produced. I really believe for my son, his friends, and all the brown young boys all over the cities, this wreaked havoc on their mental state. Remember, this had been going on for several years. I know for sure my own son's mental state was compromised because of all the arrests, all the time for BS. He eventually dropped out of high school and started hanging out with the wrong people, which led to him being arrested for real crimes. I feel he was like, *"If I keep getting in trouble for no reason, I might as well go all out and get arrested for a reason."* His record was so long for unnecessary arrests before he even hit 18. His efforts to try and do good and the right thing was going against him in the world of corruption. His mentality definitely shifted. I personally saw the change in him. I really think the "Stop and Frisk" era led him to the life he eventually started to live. He has since gotten his GED and cleaned up his life, but at what expense? All the time and years wasted, still trying to find a good job to provide for his family. It's hard out there for transformed felons, but he has overcome the odds that were stacked against him, and I am confident in his future. If I know God, everything is done on purpose and for His reason. So I have hope and a prayer that all wasn't lost. By the grace of God, my son is still standing strong.

When my son started being harassed by the police, I didn't understand what was going on. I was confused at first and then anger set in. Anger and frustration because my son was helpless and there I was, the one who protected him his whole life, unable to do anything. I felt like a total failure as his mother. Then to top it off, at first no one believed me. No one, meaning other people who didn't live in our type of neighborhoods. I would tell my co-workers in the civilian world and my fellow comrades in the Army. Either they lived in neighborhoods where this wasn't happening like Long Island or upstate New York, or they didn't have teenagers. Apparently police were targeting only our teenage boys, not the grown men. There were no camera phones to capture it back then, so for some time people thought I was making things up. Some said my son had to be doing something to get treated that way. I was really frustrated because they were calling me a liar when I said he was just walking down the block to the store, minding his business, or coming into our building to come home, or eating in McDonald's. These that I listed were just a few, but he had many stories and arrests and no one believed me. In the beginning, I felt so alone except for my immediate family being with us through it all. My son was always in trouble for something beyond his control and I couldn't help him. Our hope was on a thin string. Then I found out it was in some other New York City neighborhoods and I felt better knowing it wasn't just my son and his friends. I just prayed harder to have the madness cease. It took a while, some years later to be exact, before they took the law away or at least ended the "Stop and Frisk." Glory be to God for all the rest of our little boys growing up behind my son. Maybe they will have a better chance in life instead of a bogus rap sheet determining their future for them.

Although I did not endure as much trauma as my son, I experienced hopelessness and despair as I feared for my son's safety and well-being. Worrying if he would make it home, not just from crimes and gangs but from the very ones who were supposed to keep our children and communities safe. Wondering everyday if he would be arrested again. Would my mom or I have to show up to get him out of the precinct again?

NYPD Raid

Would the cops assault him again and get away with it the next time? And knowing I felt that way, how much worse did my son feel? How much more damage did it do to his mind, heart, and soul? My family and I never ceased praying. This is why this is my story, indirectly. It wreaked havoc on me mentally and spiritually, too. I thank God for His grace and protection over my son during that time because yes, it could have ended worse than it was, especially during an era when there were no cameras. But yet, My God kept my son guarded by angels. Only so much was allowed to touch my son. Maybe God intended for this to be my son's testimony someday as well. I don't doubt God. He knows what He's doing.

YACHT PARTY

I will praise thee with my whole heart: before the gods will I sing praise unto thee.

Psalm 138:1 (KJV)

Well well well... here is the be-all and end-all.

All the years of **heavy** drinking since I was a teen, from 1989. And here it is 2020.

You know about my extensive years of drinking. But to what extent and depth? Here's some insight to get you to understand. I started my heavy drinking in my early teens. During those years and into my early 20s, I was passing out everywhere in public places, amusement parks, snowstorms, parades, house parties, always waking up somewhere unknown from passing out drunk. I woke up to burns, bruises, and cuts all over my body, trying to figure out how they got there and how I got home. My life was the story of the movie *Hangover* before it actually came out. I was always having to piece together my previous night. Did I shame anyone? Do

Yacht Party

anything stupid? Say anything I wasn't supposed to? Offend anyone?

In my 30s to 40s, most people around me who were not immediate family, close friends, or anyone I dated had no clue I was an alcoholic. I got hip to keeping it discreet. I became what is called a "closet drinker" literally and figuratively. If I did drink out in public, I already had a plan in place to escape and make it home to continue drinking until I passed out at my own place, or I wouldn't drink at all around people. There were times I would go to job parties, etc., and just not drink until I got home.

There is a difference between drinking and being a drunk, a difference between passing out and blacking out. I did all of them. I tried drinking just my limit or just the minimum of one or two drinks. I would acknowledge and feel the buzz, tell myself to stop, but then would keep going until I blacked out and/or passed out, then wake up the next day confused. Being a closet drinker kept me from the shame of others witnessing what I could not remember the next day. I know it was harder on my kids and then my husband when we married. They witnessed it all and more because when I was teen, there were no hangovers. As I got into my 20s with my young kids, the hangovers would last maybe one day. As I got older, the hangovers would last two and three days. Who do you think took care of me and my hangovers all my life, especially when it was just my kids and me living together? They were professionals in knowing how to take care of hungover mommy, which is nothing I'm proud of at all!

I have so many drunk stories throughout the years. Let me run down some of my crazy and near-death experiences. These are just a few off the top of my head, but the list goes further:

- Drinking red wine out of Pepsi cans with straws at work and when traveling on the New York City

subway trains. Red wine so the color looked dark like the soda and no one could tell the difference through the straw.
- Flooding a co-worker's apartment and it going downstairs to her neighbor's apartment. They were already beefing, so I made things worse between them.
- Running around my block drunk and butt naked with our family dog. Ended up falling in a pot hole, scarring my knee badly to the white meat, and had a limp for days.
- Waking up in a hospital. Found out I passed out in my neighbor's yard while walking home from somewhere drunk. I almost made it back into my house safely, but not quite. They called the ambulance.
- Taking back my liquor I gave as gifts to people at their parties after I already handed it to them to have more drinks at home. More like stealing my gifts back when they weren't looking. I figured with all the liquor gifts they received, they wouldn't miss mine.
- Hiding extra liquor bottles in my closet in shoes and clothing pockets so my family wouldn't know I had extra stashed for drink emergencies when they thought I ran out. This was way after my drug addiction days and is how I was the literal "closet drinker." I was literally taking shots in my closet and hid the alcohol again.

These are some examples of stories from my more than 31 years. Let me now share my last big drunk story.

I have a bestie named Jennifer. Jenni threw her birthday party on a yacht at the marina on the river in New York City.

Yacht Party

I'm a girl afraid of water. No pool, no beach, no water above my ankles but, of course, to bathe and shower. If it's above my knees, I'm not getting in at all. But it was my girl of more than 40 years. This was my maid of honor's birthday, so I had to be there, right? I asked the captain what happened if we fell in the water for those who didn't know how to swim because they didn't give us life vests. The guy laughed and informed me no one would fall in. *"Ok, if you say so, I believe you."*

The party went on the whole day and night. It was a great party for me, but probably not so great for the girls. I talked their ears off the whole day from being drunk. Usually, I would start drinking out somewhere, then make my way home before I got too drunk for anyone to notice, then finish getting drunk at home cuz a party ain't done with me until I'm passed out in my home with my closet drinking. But I couldn't escape that day. I was on the yacht all day. Drinking ALL DAY! Surpassing my limit, as usual. I know when it was time to leave, those girls were probably happy and ready to get away from me. I talked so much my own voice was starting to get on my nerves, lol. All day we partied, ate food and birthday cake, drank, danced, and took pics. It was lit, and then it was time to go home.

I guess I put it out in the universe earlier because later that night, leaving to go home, everybody got off the yacht and we started walking down the boardwalk to our cars. They made a right turn to continue down the boardwalk. I was feeling numb and seeing blurry. I saw them make the turn, but my body wouldn't move in their direction. I just kept walking straight forward. I felt myself hit the water, heard the splash, then heard the screams muffled and faded above my head, but I still didn't know what was going on. Finally, the cold water jerked me awake. It was a delayed reaction but when I became alert, I felt myself sinking in slow motion.

The Angels Are Watching

My first thought was, "O sh!t. *This water is cold.*" My second thought was, "*I'm gonna die. I don't know how to swim.*" I calmly felt myself sinking lower and lower and did not panic or try to stay afloat. Surprisingly, I just let myself be. Going down, I didn't fight the water so I don't know why I was going down instead of floating. I could hear people screaming around me more clearly. I could hear actual words of what they were saying. Then I felt someone pulling me out of the water. It was that same captain and he was **pissed** off! I was fully alert now, sopping wet and cold. I almost died and all I could think about was that he probably thought I did that to him on purpose. I promise I didn't. I don't know why my body didn't move to make that right turn with everyone else, but I'm sure that's what it looked like to him after we specifically had the talk about no one was going to fall in the water. And it was not just me wet. He was fully clothed and soaked. At least I had on a bathing suit. I don't remember if I ever thanked him. I would hope to think I did because he saved my life. Another angel in disguise.

I was semi-embarrassed with everyone around me, but I was also too drunk to really care at that moment. We all continued to go home. The next day was the first time I ever thought of the consequences of my drinking. I thought about how I could have really died and left my kids without a mom, and that hurt me the most. Of all the years of drinking and accidents, this was the one that really hit home—the one and only time I EVER felt like my kids would be lost without me. Lost without having their mother due to my selfishness and drinking excessively that could have caused my own early death. It really made me depressed for the next few days to think about them having to live without me because of my stupidity. I always knew my drinking was a problem, but that was the first time my eyes were opened and I saw how it affected those around me and not just myself. It was the first time I felt convicted about leaving my husband and children behind because of my drinking. It was the first time I prayed to quit, not for me but to get closer to God. So I quit again. That time I meant it. It was Friday, August 14, 2020. On August 17, I wrote a message to myself in my phone calendar:

> **SOBRIETY. I will try again with God on my side!**
>
> **Fell in the river. Could've drowned. Husband and kids wouldn't have a wife/mom.**
>
> **Sobriety to get closer to God in spirit.**

I will give thanks and praises to God with my whole heart because like many of my other stories, I should've been dead but here I am, still alive.

FINDING JESUS
20

But you, be sober in all things, endure hardship, do the work of an evangelist, fulfill your ministry

2 Timothy 4:5 (BSB)

To understand this chapter, you need to know I converted to Islam during my time in basic training in 2011. I was a Muslim for nine years. So the second question I'm always asked is what made me convert back to Christianity so late in life? The transition occurred in 2020, starting in August.

After the yacht incident, you would think that would have ended my drinking but guess what? I still continued. One thing I can tell you from experience: It is not easy to quit anything, even when you know it's bad for you. Most people used to say to me, *"You can quit if you really tried."* Really? It's just that easy to quit something that is an addiction?? What's your addiction? Eating too much junk food or sweets? Drinking too much soda or coffee (caffeine)? Too much time on social media or binge watching shows? Smoking cigarettes,

Finding Jesus

vaping, weed, taking pain killers, playing video games on your phone or on a gaming system, shopping online or in person, promiscuity, pornography, gambling, placing blame on others all the time (always playing the victim), being a pessimist or a person who's always negative? The list goes on. These may not be your habits or addictions but trust me, everyone has one that's hard to break, and alcohol is no easier when you're an alcoholic. Drinking alcohol and being an alcoholic are two different things. So there I was drinking again, much less and not excessively to where I was blacking out and having hangovers. I was on my best behavior since the boat incident. In a matter of time, however, I would be right back in my never-ending cycle of addiction. So I was drinking less but drinking nonetheless, still asking God to help me quit. Why couldn't I just quit?

I fell into a mini-depression. I was just upset with myself and sad that I was still drinking when I knew I wanted to stop. This time was really different. I felt it. I was actually scared for the first time that I would leave my children motherless. So why couldn't I stop? My mind wanted to stop but my body kept craving the alcohol. The mini-depression is when I said to myself, *"I need to hear a Word from Allah."* I needed my Quran to comfort my soul. I just wanted to feel soothed and comforted. I just need to read something from You Allah, anything! Yes, I became a Muslim and was still drinking. Don't judge me. I hadn't been to the mosque in a couple of years, and I didn't do my five prayers (salat) a day anymore. I still did my prayers on my prayer rug twice a day with my head covered, but only on days I wasn't drinking. So what was I really doing? I still didn't eat pork and still called Him "Allah." I went into my night stand drawer to get my little bedside Quran. Hmmm, it was not there. I went to look for my big one that I kept in my bedroom as well. Hmmm, it was not there. I went around asking my husband and kids if they knew where either one was at. They all said no. I was upset because they didn't just get up and walk out by themselves...oh boy, I sound like someone's mother. Perhaps my own, lol. I was trying to remember the last time I actually read it. It had been a few months. I thought it would show up somewhere soon but in the meantime, I stayed in my little funky depression. It was not a full depression, but my heart was definitely heavy.

A couple days went by, literally two, and I had to look for a document needed for who knows what, at this point I don't remember. I knew it was in a big, black garbage bag in my storage closet with bags and boxes that I never unpacked when we moved into our new home in New Jersey six years prior. As I was rummaging through the bags, what did I find? My Bible. My Holy Bible. Not the one that I was reading in North Carolina when I was getting clean off drugs, but another one I had bought myself while living in Georgia. I was not excited to see it, but I was surprised to find it in that bag. I had forgotten all about it. Forgetting what I was looking for, I went to sit with it in my lap. I prayed that I would receive a word to comfort me. Any word. My heart was still heavy and I just wanted to read anything that would lift my spirit. I didn't know what to read. So once again, I opened it to a random page.

I absolutely do not remember what I read or what book of the Bible it was in. But I kept reading, and reading, and reading... and started crying. Whatever I was reading was touching my heart. It was jumping off the page and speaking to me. I cried some more. I couldn't understand how, after all those years, after reading the Quran, these words were ministering to me differently. Once again, the Bible came through and did its job, comforting me as it had the same night I read it on my last

Finding Jesus

day of drugs. What an overwhelming and beautiful feeling. It was what I had been missing. Reading the words made me feel so lightweight, like I was floating. I was so at peace, and I just kept wanting more, so I kept reading more. Everyday. I got to the point I was taking my big physical Bible to work. At that time, I didn't know about the online Bible apps. It was 2020, but when was the last time I had been around church people, the Bible, or anyone reading the Bible? Your girl hadn't heard of such a thing yet. So I was lugging my big King James Version Study Bible to work—it was huge—with my nursing supplies and my lunch. Every night like clockwork.

By this time, I had left the nursing home with the geriatric patients and was doing overnight home care with pediatrics. My patients had severe illnesses with trachs, g-tubes, and such. I was one-on-one with my patients and because of the one-to-one, this allowed me to do some reading and studying between treatments and when my patient was asleep.

I was new to reading the Bible. I grew up in the church but didn't know anything other than what I was told. I was taught to read the Bible and had read it throughout my life here and there. But this time, I was actually reading to try and learn something. I wasn't understanding anything! By the end of 2020, there were no open doors to churches because of the pandemic. I absolutely had no one to go and talk to about what I was reading. I couldn't find a church home to join, and I didn't know anyone who could help me understand. That's when I found the whole Christian community on YouTube. I happened on there by accident while Googling a word or scripture from my Bible. Once I got a hold of YouTube, it was my new best friend. I went from trying to understand the Bible on my own to a whole new world online. There I was, working the night shift, reading my Bible, listening to sermons and

Bible studies online, praying in the dark, all while in-between treatments with my patients. I just couldn't get enough. My soul and my spirit were happy again. And that's how it all started. I had so much zeal and passion. I was revived.

Before that time, the only people online I had heard of were Bishop TD Jakes and Creflo Dollar. I found them on YouTube and started listening to them. They led me to Pastor Sarah Jakes Roberts, who led me to Stephanie Ike. Somewhere along the line, I found Priscilla Shirer and Cornelius Lindsey, who led me to his wife, Heather Lindsey. One of them was on my rotation every night at work. I would listen to them, then do my own studying. I started learning how to gain knowledge and understanding of the Word. What they all had in common was the same steps of how to study the Bible on my own. I didn't need to be a scholar. All I needed was a relationship with God and He would give me revelation of His Word. All I wanted was to understand what I was reading. Before finding them, I was all over the place, just picking random scriptures that didn't mean anything to me, without understanding. What did I need to do? I followed their steps, did my research, and started with the book of John. There were many reasons why I chose that book, but mainly because it was said that to really know and understand Christ's love for us, start there. That is what sent me down rabbit holes. I started with a notebook, and my God! The joy I was getting. Spilling over to studying at home during the day, I barely got any sleep. I spent hours in the Word. I would say, *"Ok I'll just do one hour."* Next thing I knew, I was three to four hours in. I just could not get enough, but I was a baby crawling.

It took me literally months before I finished John. Every time I read one line, I was Googling everything and cross referencing between my two study Bibles. Yes, I had ordered the New International Version (NIV) so I had that and the King James Version (KJV) study Bibles. And I had to start from scratch. I even had to look up the 12 disciples. Lord forgive me, I didn't know all of them, not even all of their names. I hadn't even heard the names of all the books of the Bible like I thought I had. And to top it off... I thought every chapter in the book of Psalms was written as Psalms instead of each chapter as a Psalm with the collective book known as Psalms. I had been saying that wrong my whole life, not to mention other things I should have known. These were the least of them. How embarrassing for a girl who grew up a preacher's kid in the church. I took the time to learn about each one of the disciples, their genealogy and locations, what their names meant, their former careers before they followed Jesus, their habits, their characters, one by one, the five Ws (who, what, where, when, and why). Not much was getting read in the book of John because I got sidetracked every single time. Finally done with researching one thing, I got a little further and then, down the rabbit hole again cuz I was researching something else that sparked my interest. I had so many questions about each sentence with no one to help answer them. So I was cross-referencing between Bibles and researching (is it really research if I'm Googling?) I was like, *"Forget this, I know nothing!"* So I went on christianbook.com to order *Know Your Bible*, a cheat sheet by Paul Kent and Value Books. I ordered a kids' Bible trivia flashcard set. I didn't know many of those trivia answers either!!! Not even from growing up in Sunday School, but I never got discouraged. I just yearned for more knowledge. I prayed to God for more knowledge and wisdom every day. Every time I got an answer after thoroughly dissecting and researching the answer, I wrote it down and continued to the next trivia question. Writing it down helped me to remember so the next time I got around to that same question, I would know the answer and the five Ws. Just like I had no clue about the Bible online apps, I did not know about the trivia online apps. Now I use both hard copies and online apps to read the Bible and answer trivia questions.

It took me a while to get through the book of John, and I had a lot of *"Wow"* moments. I was getting my momentum going and eventually found out that two people I personally knew were holding Bible studies through technology during the COVID era. One of them I grew up with in the church with our families when we were both young and made to go to church. My dad and his mom were both preachers. He is the overseer at his church in the Bronx. As we became adults, he officiated my wedding and did Christian dedications for my children and nieces. Bishop Austin held his Bible studies via social media Lives on Instagram and Facebook. And Momma Loretta, aka Apostle Stewart, was a pastor who held her Bible studies via conference call lines in Georgia and then eventually on Facebook Live. Thank God that out of the tragic pandemic, new ways of technology were birthed and helped the Christian community to connect. When I found out I was able to join their studies, I split my tithes between them since I didn't have a church home, as this was still during the pandemic and I couldn't go out to find one. It felt good to have a close connection with people I actually knew who I could learn from on a personal level.

I continued listening to all the YouTube sermons to hear God speak to me. That's all I wanted. I had a deep desire to hear from God. What did I need to do? Would He really talk to me? Until that point, I only thought He spoke to His prophets, pastors, and preachers. But nope, they all said the same thing: God talks to every single one of us. If we have a personal

Finding Jesus

relationship with Him, we will be able to hear Him. Seriously? I didn't know what that meant at the time, the part about having a relationship with Him. But I wanted God to speak to me because I had questions I needed answered. I know **now** that's not how He works, lol. But again, what did I have to do? All the sermons I listened to lined up with one another every time. I was thinking, *"Wow! This is just for me. How does God know what I needed to hear?"* There were so many sermons online, I couldn't keep up. So every night, I prayed that God would send me the exact Word that I needed to hear, and He never failed to deliver. Every single time.

The yacht party was in August. I started reading the Bible again by accident and then deliberately started studying the Word by the end of August through September. In October, I was still in the book of John. Truthfully, I never thought I'd ever finish John because I was dissecting everything. But on October 15, 2020, there at work overnight in one of my patient's homes after listening to another sermon, I don't remember whose, I was finally prompted in my heart to give my life back to Christ. I believe it was either Bishop Jakes, Creflo Dollar, or Priscilla Shirer. I just repeated after the person and when I finished, I cried like a newborn baby. It was so much snot and tears, I had to clean myself up afterward in the bathroom. That whole time with every preacher saying to repent and confess **Jesus as my Lord and Savior** for my salvation at the end of their sermons, it never dawned on me that I, personally, had to because I had done so many years ago before I became Muslim. I didn't think it was for me. I had forgotten I had taken the Shahadah for Islam since I was last a Christian. But that night, my spirit spoke to me, and it was the right time for me. I repeated the words softly, in a whisper, not to wake my patient. And what a beautiful feeling.

That is my testimony of giving my life back to Christ so late in life. By myself, sitting in someone else's home. Now isn't that something? Why would God allow me to do so there, of all places? And that specific patient? That is something I am praying will be revealed to me. So what made me convert back to Christianity? I want to say it was by accident because I couldn't find my Quran til this day. But the Lord placed the Bible back into my hands. No big rock-bottom story, but a powerful story nonetheless. Or maybe I should say it was divine intervention from God because after I invited Jesus to be my Savior, everything started opening up for me. In that very home was the first time He spoke to me. That very morning—it was my overnight shift but after midnight—my spirit prompted me to go on a fast.

That was on the 15th. The very next night at work on the 16th, I was reading the Bible but not John because I didn't want to go down the rabbit holes that night. My brain needed a break. A sermon I had heard previously prompted me to read 1 Samuel 3. I closed the Bible and just recited over and over again: *"Here am I. Speak Lord, for thy servant heareth."* Over and over again. I said it with such anxiousness and despair and anguish and confidence. Then He spoke: *"You are Evangelist Keka."* God called me Evangelist Keka—in an audible voice. And I, scared at what I heard, told Him, *"No!"* That was not what I wanted to hear. What I really meant was, *"No, You can't be right. You got the wrong person."* But it came out as just *"No"* because I was startled and scared because that was the first time I heard Him speak. It was so clear and I knew exactly who was speaking. I was scared because I am nobody's evangelist. O-kay! Truthfully, I had to Google exactly what it was to get clarification. How different was that from anyone else in the church? And why would He call me that? Remember, I was a baby in Christ and

Finding Jesus

didn't know the difference between the positions and titles. All I knew about were pastors and only that they're over their congregation. That's not saying much. I knew nothing specific about the difference between apostles, prophets/prophetesses, evangelists, teachers, preachers, bishops, ministers, or any other titles. I just thought they all preached. I told Him *"No"* because I thought it meant I had to preach. I know, how dare I tell God no, but I ain't no preacher. That was the end of the conversation. He called me Evangelist Keka and I told Him *"No."* My first ever conversation with Him and it went like that. How embarrassing.

After all that desperation to hear God speak to me—and I was sure that was Him speaking—I decided to go back and forth, playing the mind game with myself. *"God, was that really you? Or was that me? Or was that the devil?"* That went on for a while in my head. Eventually, I concluded it was indeed Him. Why? Because Bishop Jakes and Creflo Dollar repeatedly preached that the devil always gives you something easy that you like and is no good for you. God will give you something that will make you uncomfortable but will help you grow in Him, in Christ, and in righteousness. It was the discomfort that convinced me it was God. But just to be clear, you must also pray, go into scripture, and/or wait for the Holy Spirit for confirmation, which is what I also did. You must never just take self or man's word for God speaking to you.

I tried to clear my mind and my shaking body because my thoughts were still, *"Please don't call me to preach. I can't do it. I am not capable. I mean, I don't even know all the books of the Bible yet, let alone what's in-between the pages."* I was literally reciting the books every day before my study so I could memorize them in order. And He wanted me to preach? I don't want to feel stupid in front of people. How am I going to teach people if I don't know myself? And the people who do know Your Word would look at me like I was a fool. *"I know You know people more equipped for the job,"* I thought *"This.Job.Is.Not. For.Me. God, please no. Don't make me do it. I am scared. I can't do this. I don't like being the center of attention. I don't like speaking in front of a large crowd or gathering. I CAN'T speak in front of a large crowd. I don't have good public speaking skills. I'm not the girl for you. Of all things, I asked you to speak to me...and this is what you tell me?"* Mind you, He didn't say I had to preach. He just called me Evangelist Keka. But there I was, overthinking and freaking out.

Disclaimer: I understand what evangelism is now. It is not necessarily to preach in the pulpit or a big platform or in front of a crowd, but simply to **speak or teach** about the gospel, the goodness of Christ, and His saving grace to the people around me, as I'm doing now or even in places where there's one-to-one conversation. It involves bringing others closer to Christ by sharing knowledge of the Son of God who died for our salvation so they can repent for the forgiveness of their sins and have eternal life with our Father in Heaven. Like seriously, who wouldn't want that? And just note, "anyone" who speaks of Christ and salvation to others who are the "lost sheep" are evangelists. There is nothing else to it. Simple as that. Most of us are doing the work of evangelism naturally without even realizing we're doing it. In my eyes, it's not even necessarily a title but a way of being and living.

I didn't realize that by saying *"No,"* I was running away from my assignment. Trying to calm my mind and spirit down from the fear that night, I listened to a random sermon from Bishop Jakes. In the sermon I chose, he spoke about when God calls, just say yes! That's it. That was the message. I was blown away.

Right message, right on time. Don't worry about not being smart enough or not equipped for the assignment. God will train you for what He asks of you. If He's calling me to it, He will see me through it. So what did I do? Right then and there, I cried and said *"Yes."* I just kept repeating, *"Yes Lord. Thank You for choosing me. I'm sorry for telling you no, for you are my Father and I am the child. My answer is yes! I'm still scared, but my answer is yes. I must be obedient to my Father. Even if I have to do it scared."* I was more afraid at that stage in my life to know Christ but still be disobedient to my Father. That is not righteousness. I was called to be an evangelist for God. Old things removed, all things anew. It was not about me anymore but the glory of God.

The day I gave my life back to Christ, I asked God to show me how to fulfill my purpose for Him because I was tired of doing things my way. I had 44 years of doing it my way. I just wanted peace. I was ready to do His Will, His way. How fast we forget when our prayers are not answered the way we expect. I said *"Yes,"* and that was the end of that.

Thinking I got over that scare, sometime in the next two days again while working, I was deep in fervent prayer and God told me to start holding Bible study. Told me right there in the quiet of the room. That's all that was said. He was on a roll that week. It wasn't said externally that time but in the quiet of my spirit. I was sure He wasn't talking about with myself because I was already doing that on a daily basis. I was totally confused because that was the second time I heard God speak to me and so soon. God was working on me fast, but I still wasn't used to hearing Him speak to me. I have to pause here and explain that it actually wasn't God speaking to me that second time. It was the Holy Spirit. Now I can decipher and know the difference between the two. In my mind, I was thinking holding Bible study meant via online or conference call like Bishop Austin and Apostle Stewart. The anxiety and fear kicked into high gear again and I was talking myself out of it, running away from my assignment once again. Because to be seen talking with my face lopsided, from Bell's palsy, was a fear I always had.

The preachers I listened to online always spoke about how to discern the voice of God. I had to get confirmation backed by scripture. Again, I chose a random sermon to listen to that night. Priscilla Shirer started preaching about ministering wherever you are. Again I heard that you don't need a grand scale, you don't need a pulpit. Start with what you have. Work with what you have. Minister on your job, at your school, in the checkout line at the store, hold Bible study in your home with your family, with your children. Bingo! Ok God/Holy Spirit, You were speaking to me. But what does this mean? I was not looking to do all that. I wasn't even sure how to hold a Bible study. I mean, I had listened in on a few, but being over it and teaching the Word? Nah, I'm good. I was just trying to be closer to God and have this intimate relationship I heard of that I wanted so badly because of the peace and the promise I kept hearing it gives. I repeated the same speech:*"I am not equipped to handle what You want me to do. How can I teach others about You if I barely know anything myself? I'm still learning. I'm still in the book of John. The first book I started TWO MONTHS AGO! I'm still in it!!! And to think I read it every day."* But then I stopped short and remembered to just say yes. I said, *"Yes Lord, just show me how."*

PER God's instructions and my obedience, weekly family Bible study in my home with my husband and children started October 21, 2020. Here's a few tweets of how it was going up until I left on my deployment in 2021.

Finding Jesus

Tweets:

October 21, 2020

"1st Bible study in my home with husband and children earlier tonight. How did it go?... Well God had me tell them what He wanted them to hear tonight. That's all that mattered. Baby steps for me. But I was obedient... it's a start."

March 15, 2021

"Family Bible study is going very well. For the 1st time, my 15-yr-old son was engaging, talking, asking questions. God answers prayers."

April 05, 2021

"My 15-yr-old just volunteered and prayed us out of our family Bible study for the 1st time. That is all!"

[The memory post on my first Bible study post - Oct 22, 2021]

"Whew! I remember this day. But God! He brought me a long way on my spiritual journey. And I'm nowhere done yet. My ministry is flourishing and I'm taking everyone with me. Family and Friends. Just believe in the Trinity (the Father, Son, & Holy Spirit) and we can help build God's Kingdom together. Blessings to all!"

Back to December 7, 2020, at work overnight. I prayed so hard and for so long to quit drinking again. Yup, again. I was still drinking all of that time following the yacht party four months prior, but definitely not as much. I was down to about once a week because I would not dare drink while reading God's Word, and I was in His Word every single day. I had too much respect for Him to do that. But I would still pick one day a week to "unwind." Even though I wasn't overindulging, it was really messing with my spirit, which was because of "conviction" because I was new in Christ. I really didn't want it anymore, but again my body kept craving it. No matter what tricks I tried, I.Could.Not.Stop. But that night, I continued praying. I had just drank the night before on my day off. Back to work, in the Word, I paused and said an unexpected prayer. This time I told God: *"You said if I ask in Jesus' name, it shall be given unto me. And that Your Word would not return unto You (null and) void. So I'm asking you to cure me of alcoholism, through your Son, Jesus, I repeat, IN JESUS' NAME. Amen."* I know I mixed the two scriptures. Then I spoke like it was done. I was really learning from the online preachers. They would say, Speak from the end like it's ALREADY done. Praise Him because it IS already done, and be Confident that it WAS done. *"I am done! I am healed from alcohol. And I am delivered through Christ Jesus. Finally!!! Amen."* And God responded, **"On the other side of that drink is your purpose,"** speaking to the fact that I would never drink again. I asked God for revelation. His answer? That was the last day my body ever craved or desired an alcoholic drink.

> **And He said to her, "Daughter, your faith has made you well. Go in peace, and be healed of your affliction."** Mark 5:34 (NKJV)

Nothing had helped me beat alcohol for more than a few months. Not all the in-patient and out-patient sobriety and rehab clinics I signed myself up for and attended throughout the years after that 30-day drug rehab stint. I was really trying to quit and help myself break free of the sickness. All the AA meetings throughout my life, nothing helped until I asked for deliverance the right way.

Finding Jesus

I asked differently that time. I asked for deliverance *"in Jesus' name."* That was the key... JESUS. And that's when He opened the door and started showing me my purpose, slowly, a little at a time. I'm being obedient every step of the way. Once I complete one assignment, He gives me another. Where I'll end up, I don't know. But I'm trying to enjoy the journey as much as possible. I figure if I did 44 years of my life doing what I wanted to do, I at least owe Him 44-plus years doing His will. And that, I am committed to do.

On my anniversary date (December 7, 2020), I wrote a note to myself in my phone calendar, and put it on repeat to remind myself every year:

> *"QUIT DRINKING IN JESUS' NAME! AMEN. Day 1 @44 yrs old. AFTER 31 YEARS OF HARD DRINKING (started drinking in 1989 at 13 yrs old, the summer between JHS & HS.)*
>
> *He said when I ask in Christ's name, it shall be given unto me. I asked and so it is so. I am done. I am healed from alcohol. And I am delivered through Christ Jesus. FINALLY!!! This date is my final anniversary date for all to be fruitful and multiply. I CAN NEVER DRINK ALCOHOL AGAIN!!! This is it! Hallelujah and Amen.*
>
> *I am no longer a drunk. I am no longer an alcoholic!*
>
> *I know for sure, I can't touch another drop of alcohol because HE told me, on the other side of that drink is my purpose. God has called me and I MUST, I must (obey and) fulfill my purpose! Hallelujah and Amen!"*

I was so ecstatic. I really felt it was different that time, but I always thought that in the beginning. I still got a lot of side eye, eye rolling, and *"We'll see how long it'll last this time"* from others, but I really did feel the shift right away. I felt lighter and freer but I was still skeptical because I always relapsed. I counted each day as it went by, like I always did, just to see how far I would get. But get this, my body didn't desire alcohol whatsoever. Alcohol was still in my home and people still drank around me wherever I went, but I had no desire. All the times before, I would quit but it was a struggle because I still wanted it and had to fight off the urge until I couldn't fight it any more and relapsed. I would go to the restaurants and order mocktails, just to feel like I was part of the "drinking" group. But this time around, I always ordered water or soda and never got the urge to order a drink. I still haven't since that first day, and now I'm two years sober. The difference this time was calling on the name Jesus and being confident in His Word that it was done! How powerful is that? It is said when you keep doing the same things and keep getting the same results, try something different. I did that time. I called on the name of Jesus!

Fast forward a couple of weeks later at work again and He spoke. God said, "*Write your stories down.*" I asked, "*What stories?*" "*Your stories. The stories of your life. And I will make them into a TV mini-series.*" "*What you mean a mini-series? For who? For what?*" Silence. End of conversation. This was the conversation between me and the Almighty, with Him speaking internally and me speaking externally back to Him. Well, your girl was feeling crazy. "*My stories. My life is called stories?*" I was more fixated on that than what he was asking of me. So I forgot about that conversation, but day by day, He would remind me of something that happened in my life and I was compelled to write it down, just to get it out of my head. It would linger in my mind all day if I didn't write it down. And I mean all day. It started with sticky notes all over my house, then a small notepad, then a big notebook, and finally a folder was made on my laptop to type them all up. The more He reminded me of the stories of my life, the more I wrote every day.

January 25, 2021. A new year. I was still working nights, still holding weekly family Bible study, and still studying on my own every day. That night I was off from work but studying in my home office. In the middle of my study, all of a sudden I had the urge to baptize myself. Why myself? Because churches were still closed and I couldn't wait. I got up, ran the water in my bathtub, and reached for oil to get ready to anoint myself before I went down in the water. What oil, you ask? Cooking oil. That's all I had. But the urge to anoint myself was real. As I stepped in the water, I prayed over the oil first. Then I asked God to understand that was all I had but what it represented for me to be before Him, the Lord. I said my baptism prayer over myself and dipped myself backwards...Ughh! How awkward was that? I came up, and it was done! I was baptized in the name of the Father, the Son, and the Holy Ghost. All of a sudden, I felt complete. Standing there by myself, sopping wet in my bathroom with the door closed, I was crying happy tears. Dear Jesus, I was so happy. I never even told my family what I did that night. Eventually, I told my husband. Then I went and ordered anointing oil on the Christian website cuz let's be honest, I absolutely cannot go around carrying cooking oil, lol. When the order came, I prayed over my oil and anointed my home, my husband, my children, and my nieces. I was on a mission, or I should say, an anointing spree.

So that was me, confessing my sins to Christ, asking for forgiveness of my sins, and accepting Jesus as my Savior. I was born again, for real. I was really trying that time around to make an effort to walk in righteousness and do God's Will. I was still learning to discern the voice of God because even though I had conversations with Him, they definitely didn't go as smooth as what you read. I had struggles understanding who was speaking. God? My own mind making up crazy stuff? The devil himself, trying to deceive me? Some of the things sounded crazy, especially when it came out of nowhere. After every conversation we had, I went into prayer and scripture or waited for confirmation. Just know that when you ask God to open up your spiritual eyes, spiritual ears, and your spirit, you will begin to see, hear, feel, and know things in the supernatural. That's what I prayed for, and that's what I got. Now He speaks to me all the time but the devil is conniving, so I have to be careful and make sure it's God. Not only does God give me instructions about what I consider to be major things, but also much of my regular day-to-day life about things that seem insignificant but are not. They always seem to eventually tie together with other bigger things. Most times, He doesn't speak to me externally. It's been a while since I last heard His voice audibly. I think it was more so in the beginning to catch my attention because as time went on, it was mostly His voice internal, quiet, and still, or the Holy Spirit speaking to me in my spirit. My confirmations would come through prayer, fasting, meditations, other people He sent, and especially through scriptures. You have no idea, until you comb through scripture, how much the Word speaks to you and through you.

At that time, I still didn't know what my purpose was or His vision for me. I was just being obedient and writing my stories down because that's what He asked of me and I'm committed to doing His Will. The importance of always giving him my *"Yes"* moved me in momentum.

February 16, 2021. Priscilla Shirer's awesome Elijah Bible study was key to my understanding of what was to come on my deployment a few months later. I absolutely can not go

Finding Jesus

on and on about how awesome that Bible study was. But I will first say, thank God that the few Christian sisters I came across and asked to study together all gave me a polite, "*No thank you.*" I figured I would learn more being around Christian women who were walking with Christ long before me. I really looked up to the women I asked. Their lights were shining in the Lord, and I wanted a piece of their light so that I could shine onto others. Given it was my first time doing any international online study, I was fearful I wouldn't keep up or understand on my own. I also asked them out of fear so they would be my crutch to lean on. When they all said no, I felt hurt and lonely. But again, thank God He knew what I needed and what I didn't need because when I tell you that seven-week study session was supposed to be almost two months, it took me four months to finish. I dissected everything and went down rabbit holes every day. I had no idea about who this Prophet Elijah was, save his name. I had my two Bibles out, my notebook, pens, pencils, highlighters, and more cheat sheets I had ordered, everything ok! By the time I was done, I had Priscilla's workbook plus my two personal notebooks full of knowledge I gained in the Word because I was deep in it. I was soooo glad those other women said no because they would've been mad at me for slowing down their pace. Actually, I wouldn't have been mad if they left me and kept moving forward without me. The simplest things had me going down them rabbit holes. Just a word or a definition would start something. "*Why was it said like that? Where did everybody else in this story come from?*" I was researching everybody's history, going down their lineages. I needed to know what their connection was to the historical story. One thing about me, I'm the "Question Queen," and I will find my answers. On top of that, I stopped to have many meditation moments, to get revelation, or just sit to bask in the presence of the Lord. It was all so powerful. I couldn't get enough of that adrenaline feeling, and it sure felt good to take my time. I was on nobody's time but my own. Thank God, each of those women told me no.

The Elijah Bible study prepared me with understanding that God was removing me away from the busy life I had known with my family and work to give me more uninterrupted study and training from Him. Being away, on my deployment, in Germany was my "Cherith," as Elijah was at the Cherith for three years during the famine and drought. I was around other soldiers, but I was still lonely. God broke me down completely to build me back up while I was out there. I mean stripped me down to shreds I never knew I had underneath all those layers of being an alcoholic all my life. I didn't even know who I was anymore, and that led into a depression, the same way Elijah ran away and sat under the Juniper tree and went through his depression. He was alone and lonely, but he had been groomed by God to fight for God and he won the competition up on Mt. Carmel. Before I left for Germany, God put in my spirit over and over again that I would be in my "Cherith" for the Lord, and I would come back a different person. I didn't understand the magnitude of what He was telling me until I was going through it. During my "Cherith," I had to keep reminding myself to wipe my tears, for it was just a season and my drought would be over soon. I was being stripped down to come out better and to fight stronger for the Lord when my famine was over. The story of Elijah helped me to get through so many days out there, that and God's reassurance that He had something better for me. Priscilla's Bible study prepared me because I could relate myself to someone else in the Bible with the loneliness and depression, and know it was just for a season.

Finding Jesus

That was my hope. If God put His prophet through it, who was I that I should go through anything less or easier? I could see I wasn't the only one who had to go through such vigorous training—and I'm not talking about anything physical—for growth in Him, my ministry, with this book, and other things. Elijah had to go through what he did so that he could stand against all the opposition of those who were against God, him, and what he stood for. I thought I had a deep connection with the study before I left on my deployment. I didn't fathom how much deeper it would get.

THE TRANSITION

Humble yourselves before the Lord, and he will lift you up in honor.

James 4:10 (NLT)

Ahhh...getting sober. The anguish, the depression, the crying, isolation, etc., all in addition to executing missions in Germany with my team. God had a bigger plan for me. It wasn't about the physicality of me being there but the spiritual, emotional, and mental training He had to give me. He had to break me down to build me back up His way.

This chapter is not about my actual missions, which would be a breach of security with the military. This chapter is instead about my spiritual transition.

I was on my deployment in Germany for about a year. That's including the time spent preparing to mobilize and time spent transitioning back home. During those months, I went through a mental health crisis. It started with depression, according to my senior leaders. The first two months there, I was good,

The Transition

participating in activities with them outside of the work day. Eventually, I slowly started staying in my barracks' room all the time outside of the missions. There are people who adopt this as their M.O., to be left alone in their rooms, but those who know me know I'm down for any socializing activities. I didn't notice the difference in my behavior as being depressed because, as I told them, I was absorbed in my own personal Bible study. I was finally able to have uninterrupted study once I was off work. No more interruptions while working overnight or once "home" in my room because I had no family to tend to. No cooking, not much cleaning, no husband and kids to take care of. I was getting my study on and sleeping. I was finally able to get more than two hours of sleep a day. Working nights and going home during the day meant I only got about a good couple of hours of sleep. I took care of the kids' remote learning online due to the pandemic and the household during the day before I had to go back to work at night. I slept those two hours when good ole hubby came home from work and took over so I could sleep before work. Being in Germany, all I wanted to do after a good work day was Bible study and sleep, sleep, sleep. To others, all that sleeping had them concerned, but I assured them I was good, just catching up on my sleep. That's the good thing about having team members who know your ways and how you move. They notice when something is off.

There I was on my off days and weekends sleeping in late and or all day. Your girl was catching up. I did not leave my room unless I had to. One day I woke up and the panic attacks started. I had never had them before. Body shaking, hands shaking, voice shaking when I talked, shortness of breath, either speed talking or forgetting my words to complete my thoughts so I would just repeat myself or not say something in mid-sentence. My voice would escalate when I repeated the same words over and over again out of frustration that I couldn't get my complete thoughts out, so it sounded like I was yelling when trying to express myself. This was going on everyday out of nowhere, and most times for no reason. Sometimes I would be talking in front of a group. I used to get a little nervous or anxious when speaking in front of people, but this was next level for me. I couldn't think straight when talking. Sometimes it would just be one-on-one with someone. Sometimes it would be me just walking down the hallway alone with no one around or in the bathroom alone. Anywhere, at any time, everyday. Most times, if I was talking with someone whether it was confrontational or not, I was in a next-level panic mode for no reason whatsoever. As a staff sergeant, it made me look as if I was intimidated by someone else, no matter the rank, in or out of uniform, and that was not the case. That was never me. Apparently that was my new normal and it started weighing on my self-esteem.

 I started losing the confidence and courage I once had. The frustration of feeling stupid and incompetent to others was making me become angry fast over petty little things that would never have bothered me before, yet I was blowing up. I was walking around like this non-speaking idiot who was always angry. Although it was obvious to others, I never let it interfere with my duties with the missions. Still, everyday I battled this war within myself. I started to not go out, not even to eat. I really had a lack of interest in everything. Day in and out, every morning I woke up, I counted down the hours until I could go back to my room and get back in bed, which I did as soon as I got in my room. I barely ate, and I would cry every single day when I made it back to my room. The self-hate was eating me up. *"Why did I sound stupid every time I had to speak to someone? Why did I even have to speak? Why couldn't I just do*

The Transition

my job without talking to others and go back to my room at the end of the day?"

I tried so hard not to talk to anyone, but that's not how life works. When you're on a team, everyone is involved on every level, especially as a non-commissioned officer (NCO). There were days I counted how many times I had said something stupid or didn't say anything because a loss of words had me stuttering or I suffered just plain ole anxiety and panic attacks, with me standing in front of someone with shortness of breath or obvious body shaking. I had so much anger and despair within myself for not being able to verbally complete my thoughts that were stuck inside my head, fighting to come out, hence the stuttering. I never stuttered in my life, but it was my new normal. I started noticing the snide remarks and snickering. I was being made fun of, discreetly, although they didn't think I noticed. And that, ladies and gentlemen, made me feel even more incompetent and stupid. My whole life, I had never known that feeling until then at 44 years old. I had always had a kind of confidence within me, but I was withering away within myself. Why did I even care at that age? I was never one to care about what anybody said or how they felt about me, but I would count every day to see if I surpassed my stupidity and panic attacks from the day before. It was an awful competition within myself. If I wasn't depressed before that, I most certainly was as time went on. Always in my room, not eating, and not even doing my Bible study. Wow! That was a significant change. All I did was go to my room, cry forever, pray to God asking Him why was I like that and for Him to please heal me of anxiety and panic attacks, and then finally fall asleep. That was my daily routine. All I did was keep asking God, "Why? Why? Why?" That was also the time I started to pull on the hope that I gained through Prophet Elijah's story, the hope to know I was just going through a season. One day, I would be back to my old self, that confident and intelligent woman I always saw myself as.

The insecurities were kicking in big time. The anxiety, panic attacks, self-hate, and the lack of confidence, courage, and self-esteem from feeling both stupid and ugly. The ugly was from the Bell's Palsy kicking in again. I'm assuming that was from the anxiety that was affecting the nerves in my face. My face started twitching all day and hard again like when I first got it back in 1999. I was self-conscious about my face and feeling so ugly that I continued to wear a face mask even after it became optional when COVID was dying down. I was the only one in the office wearing one. I told everyone it gave me warmth to my body, as like a hat on my head, since I was always cold, which was also true, but it was mainly to cover the lower half of my face from the obvious twitching my lip was doing throughout the day. My eye still twitched uncontrollably, but I figured it was better for one thing to be covered than none. I couldn't cover my whole face but trust me, I would have if I could. That all drove me into a full-fledged depression. I mean, I was still able to execute missions with no problem, but I was seen differently. I WAS A MESS! I was Elijah during his time at "Cherith." I felt alone and depressed for months. Then one day, on a break at work, I was scrolling through my sobriety Facebook group. A woman supporting her husband's sobriety listed some of his symptoms and asked the group what was wrong with him. She wanted to know if any of us had gone through what he was experiencing because she thought he was depressed but she wasn't sure. Someone answered that it was normal. He was going through his PAWS phase and she should not worry, it would pass. What was this? I Googled it and BINGO! I found out what my problem was. My own self-diagnosis.

The Transition

Post-Acute Withdrawal Syndrome (PAWS) is the second stage of detox or withdrawal symptoms that occur as the brain re-calibrates after active addiction. The first step is usually a physical, acute withdrawal lasting a few days to a few weeks with your body, i.e., the shakes, etc. The second stage is mental and emotional and can last from months up to about two years as the brain attempts to seek a healthy equilibrium. PAWS is the brain's way of correcting chemical imbalances that it suffered from during active addiction. The longer the addiction, the longer the PAWS phase. I had been sober from alcohol for a little over six months at that point, which was about the longest I had been sober after being an alcoholic for so many years. Some of the symptoms I encountered that were listed included sleep disturbances; fatigue; irritability, hostility, aggression, and other mood swings; anxiety and panic attacks; depression; impaired concentration, foggy thinking, and trouble remembering; lack of interest and motivation; poor impulse control; increased sensitivity to stress; and changes in appetite. And the list went on. I was on an emotional roller coaster that was overwhelming me. All I could do was cry out to God everyday, but I finally had a reason for my feelings and actions. The beginning of my sobriety was taking a toll on my mental and physical health as my brain and body began to heal and reorient itself after so many years of hard drinking and substance abuse.

At the same time my symptoms and depression became so intense. I didn't know who I was anymore. I certainly didn't recognize the girl I'd become. Truthfully, anybody back home would've been just as confused as me because they would've never believed me if I had told them. A different one of my senior leaders and another military personnel member noticed my symptoms and both recommended I speak to a behavioral health therapist, which is what the Army calls therapy. I obliged. I had an idea where it all was stemming from, but I still needed a way to cope and manage my emotions and feelings. The two main things that were breaking me down mentally and spiritually were the long-term drinking that messed up my word memory and the uncontrollable panic attacks. I felt so stupid that I couldn't get out of my mouth words that were trapped in my mind when talking with others. I knew what I wanted to say, but the words just would not come out and I sounded like an idiot. I was so jaded and clouded from the alcoholism that I would speak slowly or hesitantly, or not at all. Once I started seeing my therapist, I was able to get a better grip on myself, as he helped me recognize some things and make adjustments.

Once I was able to clear my mind a little better, it opened me up. It had been some months, but I was able to get back into studying the Word daily and watching YouTube sermons again. I threw in the mix podcasts by Priscilla Shirer's older sister, Chrystal Evans Hurst. She is the "Queen of Encouragement." I was revived! Then I realized God had sent help to me through therapy to open my eyes because I was too busy questioning Him instead of listening to Him when I was going through what I was facing. With my heart opened back up to receive Him, I started writing Bible scriptures and affirmations on index cards and paper, taping them everywhere in my room. Reciting them every day, I became stronger spiritually. I felt I was becoming a new person. The ways I thought, acted, and spoke became different. I was more understanding. I would let things slide that I wouldn't normally. I was very selective on what I needed to speak up on. Everything didn't need confrontation, as I was used to growing up fighting and arguing all the time. I felt like a chump a few times—oooh that was

The Transition

hard—but at the same time, I was gaining more peace because I was learning to let things go and let God fight my battles. And they were no longer just physical, as I once thought. I had begun to encounter battles in the supernatural. My spiritual eyes were being opened and boy oh boy, the demons that are around us are nothing less than what the Bible tells us. I would like to give my specific stories about my encounters, but this is not the right book to put them in. I may write another book about my personal spiritual warfare and how each time, I was able to break free. There are more stories that happened in the supernatural while I was in Germany and after I returned back home. I may sound crazy to some, but those who have an intimate relationship with God understand me. He allows us to see differently than the carnal eye.

After I repented for allowing myself to be so easily distracted and distanced from God, I started gaining His trust back. God continued to give me instructions. He told me to copyright my stories. After trying to figure out how to do it and failing, I forgot all about it. Once God told me again, it was about another two weeks before I actually figured it out. Then I got an email. A publishing company reached out to me about publishing my book. They said my book was listed with the Library of Congress. I assured them I had no book, just stories. Then it hit me. *Did God want me to write a book? Had He been telling me all along to write down my stories so they could be published as a book? But why? I thought He said a TV mini-series? So what happened to that?* After going into prayer, scripture, and fasting, I received my confirmation. Indeed, yes! That was His assignment for me at the moment. Of course, I was hesitant at first. *"God, really? I don't want anyone knowing the personal and intimate details of my life. So many secrets I held onto so as not to be looked at as a fool or ashamed. I don't want to be judged. I'm so* embarrassed about a lot of what I've been through." He told me it wasn't about me, but for the people to understand that He is the only One and True Living God who kept me all this time, and to use my stories for His glory. So I decided, *"No sweat. I'll just use 'anonymous' or a fake name."* But once again when He spoke, He told me to use Keka Samuels. I mean down to the last syllable. I was to use my childhood name. That was going to be very shameful for me, but I will be obedient and walk with my head held high because this is bigger than me. It's not about me.

After confirming that I was to write this book, He brought the title to me: *The Angels are Watching*. Those are His words, not mine. Believe me because at the time, I didn't believe in angels. I just knew they were mentioned in the Bible. I didn't know what they were or why they existed. So I was very concerned about the title. But I was obedient and the more I studied about angels, the more I understood their assignment to God and to the human race. This book was inspired by Him, titled by Him, and written by me for His people to turn their lives back to Christ and to show others that He can and will turn your pain into purpose if you allow Him. Your painful experiences are hope for the hopeless. We're just His messengers.

The first publishing house that reached out to me, which shall remain nameless, was not the right fit. But then God brought 13th and Joan Publishing House to me, and now the book has been completed. While I was putting my book together for His people, I was getting my rhythm back. I started attending Sunday church services on another military base, splitting my tithes three ways, and attending their Wednesday night online Bible study. Simultaneously, He instructed me to hold my own Bible study for the soldiers in the barracks' dayroom on Tuesday nights. Whew God! Thank you for the

The Transition

training with my family Bible study back home, cuz I still didn't know what I was doing. I just followed the pattern I had been using at home, along with using another online Bible study from Priscilla Shirer titled *Discerning the Voice of God*. I'd had an awesome learning experience from her previously, so I just continued with what I knew worked. Most Tuesdays, I would be the only one in attendance. I remember once when I almost didn't go on a Tuesday night when I knew no one would show up that week because of missions some soldiers were on that kept them away that week. I questioned why I should even go. I could just study in my room alone like I did daily. But the Holy Spirit spoke to me and told me, *"I am about my Father's business and I need to hold His Bible studies to His standard every single time. Even when no one is around or watching."* I obeyed and continued to do so, whether I was alone in the dayroom or not.

Things were going along well, and then God instructed me, when it was time to go back home, not to go back to nursing. The very thing that helped me get delivered and saved in my patient's home, he was taking from me. I struggled and cried over this for many days. How could I let this go? The one thing I was finally proud of accomplishing, besides working in broadcasting, and I had to let it go??? All those little dead-end jobs I struggled with as a single mom and then I had a real career with substance that I can retire from. I was so proud of how far I had come in life. My husband, kids, mom, and family were so proud of me. I thought I had finally found my purpose serving my local community as a nurse and serving my country as a soldier. But that was my flesh. All along, my purpose was spiritual, to praise and give God the glory and to bring people to Christ. That is my purpose. It has always been my purpose. Had I not come back to Christ, I would've missed my calling. And while I know God can place us in any position to serve our purpose helping others, mine was not in nursing.

I again asked if I was really hearing from God, the devil, or myself. More tears, prayer, scripture, fasting, and many, many, many confirmations later, I let it go. The tears were in part because nursing school was no joke. I had barely made it out alive, to say the least. All the sacrificing I and my family made for me to attend school. Then there was my pride of being called a nurse. I was in love with that title. I felt like somebody, so accomplished in my wild and crazy life. I finally did something right. I was back on track and my family was good with a two-parent and two-income household. So I said, *"Yes Lord, I hear you,"* just to acknowledge I heard Him speak to me, but I did nothing to back up my word. Absolutely nothing. Then days later, He said it a second time and I said, *"I heard you the first time."* Oooh, I was salty. So I let it go halfway cuz you know... just in case. By halfway, I meant, I promised Him I wouldn't go back, but I still paid my nursing license and liability malpractice insurance fees that "just happened" to come up right at that time. Coincidence much? No, God was testing my obedience and I failed.

A few nights later, it just so happened, I watched a Joyce Meyer's sermon on YouTube. I didn't normally watch her but you know it, God brought His message to me through her. She preached about straddling the fence with God. Either you're all in or all out. There's no halfway anything pertaining to God. Give Him our all! And she even had a fence built on the stage and had one leg hanging over it. She was really invested in us getting the message. That very night, He woke me out of my sleep and for His third and final time, He told me not to go back to nursing. That time I said, *"I got you."* The next day I resigned from my job that was being held for me when I got back home, and then I cried for days. Whew! All that crying. I asked Him what I was supposed to do when I got back home if not nursing. I had nothing else, and I had to help support my husband and family. He told me I would build a women and teen ministry. Clear as day, that was said. I gained more confidence in my decision to leave nursing and follow God's calling through the preaching of Priscilla Shirer and the knowledge I gained from her online teaching about Elijah. She stated, *"In order to get us adequately prepared for the moments to come, God may not allow us to return to the way things used to be. God needs us bold and fervent and clear of mind. He'll often call us to an in-between place."* I felt this speaking to me because I knew I wouldn't be returning to the way things used to be when I worked as a nurse. To get me prepared for things to come, specifically my women and teen ministries, He called me to my in-between place, which was Germany. I asked God how I was supposed to run the ministries. I said, *"I know nothing about these things, not even how to start them. And who's going to help me? I don't have a church home."* And then there was silence. One thing I will say is that He is consistent: When He speaks and I start asking questions, He goes silent. I guess He's saying He's the Father and I am the child, so who am I to question Him? He is also telling me not to worry about the things I questioned. In time, He always reveals the answers.

I was no longer in a complete depression, but I still had panic attacks that weren't as bad. I could tell I was getting better and things were looking up for me. I was more alive and vibrant. I kept my mind occupied in prayer, the Word, affirmations, and writing my book, but I was still lonely. I had soldiers and my team all around me, so I wasn't lonely in the physical sense, but lonely spiritually. I longed to be around other Christian women of God again, just as I had when I first came to Christ and had no women to share with in my journey or Bible studies. I just wanted others to share my love of God with and learn with and pray for one another and call about spiritual things. I still had my unofficial "spiritual mom," Momma Loretta, aka Apostle Stewart, back in Georgia. I didn't want to keep bothering her all the time, even though she said she didn't mind. I needed to balance myself out and give her a break sometimes because I definitely was calling her and asking her spiritual and scripture questions all the time. I also wanted to be in close physical contact with someone to be able to fellowship with and go out and do things together during our down time. That required someone in my location. So I was still alone on my spiritual journey, first at home, then again on my deployment. There were a few times I connected with Christian women from the church I was attending, but soon after they would re-deploy back home. There was that hope again, hope that it was just for a season and one day I'd be surrounded by my own circle of Christian sisters that God had entrusted me to and blessed me with. Don't get me wrong, I still had my girlfriends, sister, and female family members back home. But let's be honest, they'll talk about God but scriptures and spiritual warfare was another level they weren't on. Everyone's spiritual journey is at a different pace, and we weren't on the same page. Athough me and my girls held each other down with everything else, I still needed some Christian sisters for some fellowship with God and to pray with. The saying is *"No new friends,"* but new friends in the Lord are always welcomed.

While writing this book, I saw the humbling work of the Lord during my time in Germany. He used PAWS to strip me of everything I was, my confidence, self-esteem, and pride. He trained me up to start all over in Him because now I walk differently, I talk differently, I think differently, I act

The Transition

differently. I think before I speak now, I am slower to anger for the most part. I'm still a work in progress. Now I usually pray, fast, speak to God, and sleep on decisions before I react. I came out such a different person, and it's all because of Him and for Him. I'm a new creature in Christ. The only way I could make it out of my drought was by staying in His Word and in Him. Without Him, my mind was corrupted and confused by satan. Now that I know how to let God fight for me and empower me to stand up for His Kingdom, I can rest in peace knowing He'll take care of it all, just like He did for Elijah at Mt. Carmel.

I found humility attaching my name to this book and reveal my life secrets that I had held in privacy. I spared you that whole conversation I had with God. I went back and forth with God until He won. He always wins. I just need to learn to say *"Yes"* from the very beginning. I really tried bargaining with Him, wanting to write it anonymously or under a pen name. In the end, He said I was to use my childhood name. How embarrassing! I never wanted my stories told but from the very beginning, God told me it was not about me anymore. As I submitted to and obeyed Him, He freed me of my old life and blessed me with a new life. Now I strive to live righteously. I just want to hear Him say, *"Well done, my good and faithful servant."* So I submit my stories to you, His people, as instructed, with my name attached.

Because I wasn't able to humble myself before the Lord, He did it for me. Just like while I was in the Army, God broke me down in His way and trained me back up to His standard. I will say that while I wasn't cocky before, I definitely held myself to high standards. I had high self-esteem and great pride but all to my own glory, like I had been doing all the things on my own accord with hard work. I was pleasing myself instead of God. He had to show me He was in charge of my life by stripping my ego, dignity, and self-respect until I felt worthless. Who did I, in this flesh, think I was? I really thought I was doing something but no, it was all Him and by His grace alone. I did not keep myself going during those rough times. He did. Everything I thought I accomplished on my own was always Him and angel armies He sent to protect my life and not me myself. It was His deliverance that set me free after all the anguish and pain of crying out to Him day and night. Because He kept me out of my own way, I can now continue in my spiritual growth. I am ready to do the work to help build His Kingdom.

I am doing much better with my anxiety, but am still having some difficulties. I am back home in the states continuing therapy. Between God (the source) and the help He sends me (therapy resources), I have faith that a full and complete healing will come in His time. Everything in His time.

Below are two of the many affirmations I typed, printed out, and hung around in my barracks' room. The funny thing is, I would recite them daily with so much confidence and conviction, but had no idea the grand significance they had until now.

ONE:

"I was created with a different cadence in mind by God.

Walk differently.

Walk with purpose.

Walk like I mean it.

Walk without fear.

Walk like I'm headed to a destination worth going.

Walk with resolute confidence and boldness in who I am and in what I have, in Christ." - Priscilla Shirer

TWO:

WHO AM I?

I AM GOD'S DAUGHTER, Respectfully!

Made in God's Image (spiritually.) Therefore I am Courageous, Confident, Compassionate, Loving, Forgiving, Non-Judgemental, Wise, Knowledgeable (and growing/learning everyday), Humble, and Beautiful.

I am not who I was or where I've been.

I AM GOD'S DAUGHTER!

Nayo Bukeka = Nayo (we have joy) Bukeka (the pretty one) – I am beautiful inside and out because God created me. Don't ever think otherwise Ever Again!

A NATION (GENERATIONS) OF ME WILL COME AFTER ME BY THE GRACE OF GOD! THAT NASTY, DISRESPECTFUL PERSON I ONCE WAS TO MYSELF AND GOD, GOD HAS HUMBLED ME, TO USE ME. I AM BACK, UNDER GOD'S COMMAND! AND THIS TIME, I SURRENDER AND AM COMMITTED TO YOU GOD, UNTIL THE END! – Keka

MY PAIN FOR HIS GLORY

Not only so, but we also glory in our sufferings, because we know that suffering produces perseverance; perseverance, character; and character, hope. And hope does not put us to shame, because God's love has been poured out into our hearts through the Holy Spirit, who has been given to us.

Romans 5:3-5 (NIV)

Back home from my deployment, I resumed family Bible study on Tuesday nights in my home. This time around, we had a couple of guests join us from time to time—my nieces and my teenage son's friend. It reminded me of growing up in my household with my parents when my dad held Bible study in our home with our family, church members, and neighbors in the building. It seemed like my life went right back around full circle. I was right back where I started out and tried to escape as a little girl. But before I left for Germany, the struggle was real as I was trying to figure out the Bible study thing. I'm glad to say, with much participation from the family, we're doing much better and on God's timing, He has us right where He wants us.

Ultimately, God used my pain for His glory to let others know there is a God. There is no way I would have gotten this far in life without Him or His angels' protection placed around my children and me, especially when I wasn't following His path. He never left my side. He and His angels guarded me and held me up all the days I was weak. Now I'm back on the right track. I am now living a happier, peaceful, and fruitful life as promised in the Bible for those who walk in His righteousness. May He get all the glory!

Since giving myself back to Christ, I have an intimate relationship with my Heavenly Father and Jesus Christ. I'm 19 years clean off drugs, almost three years sober off of alcohol, have a happy marriage and four healthy children. Looking back over the years, I realize every time I was going through something, I prayed to Him, called on Him, and or read His Word just out of habit because that's what my parents taught me growing up. I thank God that every time, He heard my cry and rescued me. And for those days I didn't know to call on Him, He still had me surrounded and protected by His angels because of my praying parents and community.

Giving my life back to Christ and being obedient to God have re-routed my journey in life. While I thought I knew what my life was about, He had other plans for me. I started to see them unfold right before my eyes, step by step. I am starting to live a new life I never thought was possible and so far, what I'm witnessing is beautiful. And this is just the beginning walking with Christ. I am walking in my purpose now, as He has birthed a new ministry in me, Mikan Ministries, for the glory of His Kingdom.

> *Because of your partnership in the gospel from the first day until now, being confident of this, that He who began a good work in you will carry it on to completion until the day of Christ Jesus.* **Philippians 1:5-6 (NIV)**

Now that this book assignment is complete, what's next for me?

My family and I are still looking for a church home. I acknowledge that we need to have a covering over us in the church. In the meantime, while doing our weekly family Bible study, we are building upon Mikan Ministries. Dedicated to women and teens, our ministry is devoted to aiding in their spiritual development. Our mission is to serve God and enhance the Kingdom of God by serving others and saving lives on earth and eternally. We have so much work to do, and we're just getting started. This ministry is very dear to me because I remember what it felt like being alone in the streets as a teen. I was fending for my way through life, feeling alone because of my choices, even though my parents were there for me. As a young woman going into adulthood, I again felt alone as I was fending for myself and children as a single parent. We have so much planned with our ministry for women and teens to show them the true way of righteousness while addressing their domestic needs in life and empowering them to be able to live in fulfillment, purpose, and fellowship without the void of loneliness. We will also work with addicts and the Autism communities, as both groups are dear to my heart. After all that I've been through, I will use my experiences and testimonies to help others, all with the love of God.

I'm preparing to attend a Bible college to gain more knowledge of our One True Living God, who surpasses all. This is not for any title, but because I thirst for more and more knowledge and wisdom. I just can't get enough, and I pray it never ceases.

I now do my personal study with four Bibles—two belonging to my late father. I like to read the commentary he's written in them to help give me a better understanding of his thoughts. My main two Bibles are the NIV Life Application Study Bible and KJV Study Bible. Bless the Lord for study Bibles because ooh wee chile!...they have both blessed me tremendously as I learned God's Word from scratch on my own.

Instructed by God, I'm already working on my next book. It will be a 28-day more full and thorough devotional for those who choose to seek more of God and Christ. I'm waiting on God's instruction about authoring a book on my personal spiritual warfare. As you continue to live in Christ, you will have to overcome spiritual warfare. As God has His angels to carry out His works, so the devil has his demons. The devil always uses his demons to attack you or try to pull you from God's hands. I've had many attacks so far, but there are two particular stories I want to share about when I came home after deployment. In one, I and my family were under the spell of witchcraft. And the other, I was specifically sought and solicited to join a cult. Remember that nothing in this life is random. Everything is spiritual, whether we believe it to be true or not. I would like to tell my story of how God revealed both situations to me and all that I had to do to break my family and myself free from them both, as well as all the people who were involved. It went on for months but God paved the way and again, had His angels stood guard over us. If it's His Will, maybe you'll get to read about it someday. And for those who don't believe this to be true and think it's all craziness made up in my head, I understand. I was once there myself. Only when God opened my spiritual eyes and ears and my spirit to the supernatural was I able to see what the natural eye couldn't see. My encounters are backed by scripture, which had a hand in helping us break free.

More of my stories that never made it into this book will be included in *The Angels Are Watching* mini-series, including the molestation as a young girl, my attempted suicide, abortions, more Child and Protective Services bogus stories, more drunk stories, more corrupt police and law enforcement encounters, almost dying from COVID, the tragic 9/11 tragedy and me working downtown in Manhattan when everything happened, the few times I had guns pulled out on me, some of my children's stories and their perspectives... and the list goes on. The show will balance out and show a lot of good times my family and I were involved in as well. It'll be a journey, so stay tuned! God is always preparing us ahead of time, unbeknownst to us. Just like He had me start with family Bible study so I could carry out Bible study with the soldiers, God had trained me with working behind the scenes in productions and broadcasting prior, stripped me down and built me back up, just to go back to my first love with the televised mini-series. We are still shopping around for the best home for our televised series, but at least I have a better understanding and some experience to be able to help with the production of the show. Isn't God good? He knows what He be doing. Nothing is done by accident. Nothing is random or insignificant in our day-to-day lives. God wastes NOTHING! It is all in preparation and ties together for our purpose in His Glory. *And we know that all things work together for good to them that love God, to them who are the called according to His purpose.* **Romans 8:28 (KJV)**

To top it off, until the day of Christ Jesus, I will serve the Lord and teach the Gospel to His people.

God will not settle for mere acknowledgement of His existence. He wants your faith to lead to a personal, intimate, and dynamic relationship with Him.
- Anonymous

> *I keep asking that the God of our Lord Jesus Christ, the glorious Father, may give you the Spirit of wisdom and revelation, so that you may know him better. I pray that the eyes of your heart may be enlightened in order that you may know the hope to which he has called you, the riches of his glorious inheritance in his holy people, and his incomparably great power for us who believe.* **Ephesians 1:17-19 (NIV)**

You made it to the end of this book! I want to say thank you for being a part of my journey and would like to leave some final words with you.

If you yearn to hear God or the Holy Spirit speak to you, it is possible. If you yearn to receive guidance or purpose for your life in God's Will, it is possible. If you yearn to have peace and prosperity on earth and eternal life in Heaven, it is possible. It really is not a hoax. You can have it all. All you have to do is have faith and an intimate relationship with Him. And how do you do that?

1. **Seek God:** *But seek ye first the kingdom of God, and his righteousness.* Matthew 6:33 (KJV)
2. **Accept Jesus as your Lord and Savior:** *If you confess with your mouth the Lord Jesus and believe in your heart that God has raised Him from the dead, you will be saved. For with the heart one believes unto righteousness, and with the mouth confession is made unto salvation.* Romans 10:9-10 (NKJV)

3. **Ask God to open your spiritual eyes, ears, heart, and mind:** We cannot really even understand what the Word really is without God's supernatural help. *Open my eyes that I may see wonderful things in your law.* Psalm 119:18 (NIV)

You will learn how to discern His voice when He speaks and you receive revelation of His instructions when He orders your steps. Then will you be able to rejoice with the Lord forever in the final Kingdom when this physical life is all said and done. Who wouldn't want all these things, right? Who wouldn't want to try this for themselves? Especially those of us who desire to know our purpose in life. If you're not sure I'm speaking the truth, what do you have to lose? You can only gain. As transparent and honest as I've been about myself throughout this whole book, why would I be any less now? Try Jesus for yourself.

When God calls for you to do whatever, don't be like me in the beginning. Learn from me and just say *"YES"* from the start. Saying yes will give Him enough trust in you to give you your next steps in life. Remember love, patience, submission, obedience, and faith will get you far with God, who will give you what else you need to fill the gaps.

There will still be some hardships every now and then. Physical life is not something we can breeze through easily as we journey toward eternity. However, I can attest to the peacefulness and freedom you will attain as you learn to put God first in all things, good or bad. Stay in God, prayer, praise, and worship.

Remember, we are all God's children. That will never change. We're not bad people, we just may have bad habits and behaviors. That is what changes from good to bad and back again, or vice versa. Just around and around in one big ole circle. The fact you are God's child will always remain. So don't think you can never be forgiven for bad choices or behaviors you may have encountered or been involved in. You are still God's child! He will always forgive you when you ask Him, through Jesus' name. And He will always keep the protection of His angels around you. So know that you don't have to fight any battles alone. Your angels are working on your behalf to keep you safe, as God sent them to His people in the Bible, and as God kept me surrounded by them.

Remember always that you never know who is looking for light in the midst of their storm. Be the light!

Learn people so you can learn to love people. God wants us to love one another.

Continue to keep me and my family lifted up in prayer, as I do the same for you all. I'm excited to live the second half of my life, and I'm just getting started.

And last, be faithful. Don't give up. There's work to be done.

May the grace of God be with you all. Stay blessed!

Keka

LESSON I LEARNED OVERALL

    Everything we do in life has consequences or rewards. That is the vital key to decision-making.

    I was so free-minded to do whatever I wanted, not thinking of the consequences, only what I expected the outcome to be. I never weighed the options. I'm definitely not an astrologer, as it is actually forbidden in the Bible, but I do recognize that most of us Sagittariuses are alike. We are free-minded and free-spirited people who don't usually think before we speak or act, which makes us seem cold-hearted or rude at times. This is not the case. We are just speaking or acting out of pure honesty from the heart without beating around the bush, which may seem harsh to others, but it is not intentional. In our minds, we mean nothing disrespectful by what we say or do, but the delivery is most times perceived by others negatively. Although I am not responsible for the way people receive my message, I am concerned about being more considerate to others. It's something I've been working on these past few years.

    Whenever I got myself into something, I would say, *"Oh well, that's life. It can't always be perfect. Some have it easier, some have it harder."* I never played the victim or blamed anyone, not even myself. But I know now that everything bad that happened to me was because of my own poor choices made

Lesson I Learned Overall

without thinking and because of my selfish ways. I was always thinking about myself and not having consideration for others beyond my children. My mentality was, *"You do you, I do me."* My poor choices and their consequences included:

- rebellion at home that resulted in becoming a runaway and spending time in a group home
- substance abuse while pregnant that caused Bell's Palsy
- greed for a free trip to the Bahamas that put me in an extremely uncomfortable situation where I was disrespected the whole time and put in danger
- drugs again and my kids being taken from me
- riding around with extremely drunk drivers that led to my DUI arrest
- being a drunk landed me in the hospital a few times in addition to passing out in public a few times, almost drowning in a river, running down the street butt naked, losing people who I considered friends, and all sorts of additional embarrassing stories

Actually, there were only a few times in my life when I blamed myself for certain situations.

One was the rape. I blamed myself for years because I kept saying I should've never trusted him in a hotel room. What did I think he wanted? But he played it so smooth. I don't blame myself anymore. No is NO!

The second was the struggles I endured as a single parent who did not get child support or physical help from my three baby daddies. Although I don't regret my children and love them unconditionally, I did blame myself for the choices I made of who I had my children with. I accept the fact and responsibility that I should have gotten to know those men a little more. I also know you don't ever really know a person fully like you think you would. I was younger, naïve, and therefore fooled by their words and actions. Every. Single. Time. At the same time, they could've been a little more responsible. I didn't ask for child support from any of them in the beginning. I had to keep asking them for any help they could give, sometimes crying to them just to send me $20 or come see their child. Then I got tired of begging. I never had my kids just to get money, but why was I taking on all the responsibility for our child? Three baby daddies and they all knew how to beat the system except for one, who later on decided to do the right thing by paying. But I still had to do it alone because he refused to interact with his child. At the time, I wasn't aware I was always picking the same type of man: Physically and mentally abusive, drunks, and/or married, whether I had children from them or not. That was until, as I got much older, I prayed to break the cycle and found my current husband.

The third was that at first, I blamed myself for my house being robbed because I let a stranger in my home. But I realized I am a kind-hearted person who doesn't like to see any kid hungry. I still feed kids who come to me for food. Depriving a hungry child is not me. My kindness made me oblivious to the fact that the kid robbed me the first time. I had my gut feeling but no proof. Now I don't blame myself for feeding a hungry child. God knew my heart was in the right place, even though the kid robbed me twice.

Other than those three situations, I pretty much accepted my consequences as they came by saying each was a part of life. I still kept doing what I wanted to do, not thinking of life, rules, or laws.

Lesson I Learned Overall

The lesson I learned overall comes from the fact that I have matured and asked for more wisdom so that I slow down and respect the fact that everything should be thought through before acting or reacting. I was very impulsive for instant gratification during every period of my life. I'm sure a lot of the problems from my past could've been avoided, although not all. But maybe, just maybe, my life would have been a little different with less heartache and struggle. I now take my time and sometimes sleep on an answer before I give it. I say *"No"* to a lot of things after thinking of the consequences. I realize now that God has given this world standards, law, and order for us to be productive in this lifetime for a reason. It's in the Bible. I take my time to think more rationally about how something would affect God, my family, myself, my loved ones, and others. Lesson learned.

However, on the flip side, I know God gives us free will so whatever route we choose to take can either make our life's journey easier or harder. In the end, scripture tells us that *All things work together for good to them that love God.* -**Romans 8:28 (KJV)** He gave me free will and allowed my traumas without giving me too much to bear so that now I can testify to His glory that this woman is still standing. Thanks be to the only One Living God and Christ who gave me salvation so that I could do away with my old life and start anew with a fresh, clean slate. Every day is a new beginning as He gives us our daily bread. Although my old life was spent not thinking of any consequences, it was just as the Lord planned my life because here I am today, being used to speak of His Good News and glory because of those same said consequences.

Another lesson I have learned is that there is a God and He uses His angels. How else would I have made it this far? Having now come through so many difficult experiences, the advice I want to share is something I wish I had learned early on myself:

Every answer to your questions in life is in the Holy Bible. There's nothing new under the sun. The world evolves and cultures change, but God never changes. He instead changes us and how we view life and how we live. He is the same yesterday, today, and tomorrow. *The grass withers, the flower fades, but the word of our God will stand forever.* -Isaiah 40:8 (ESV)

Seeking HIS Word delivered me from drugs and alcohol and put me on the path to a better way of living and a more peaceful life. Yayyy to being clean and sober! Yayyy to sobriety! Yayyy to no more hangovers! Yayyy to walking in righteousness! I am better equipped to handle situations because I seek His Word in the Bible and give Him free Will over my life instead of living by my own free will. My advice is to put God and Jesus in EVERYTHING, especially when you want to make real changes in your life.

The lesson for you is that the Bible does more than just tell us how to get to Heaven. It is the source for a complete way of life—the Christian living way of life. His Word is vital as you seek answers, standards, law, and order just as the Bible tells it.

So go before the throne of God and seek the Lord for salvation and He will direct your path in the Christian way of living and then eternal life, through His Word and the Holy Spirit. Start now! Waiting another day may just be too late.

SALVATION PRAYER

If it wasn't for me calling on the name Jesus, God delivering me from alcohol addiction, and now having an intimate relationship with the Most Holy One, I would not be walking in my purpose today. This book would not have been written, and Mikan Ministries would not have been founded to be of service to God, His Kingdom, and His people.

There is only one way to have a personal relationship with God, and that is through Jesus Christ. Make this the day you change the trajectory of the rest of your life.

> *Did you not know that I must be about My Father's business?* —Luke 2:49 (NKJV)

If you're reading this and you've never been born again, recite this simple prayer and let it lead you to the throne of grace.

> *"Heavenly Father, I realize that I'm a sinner, but right now I repent of all my sins. I receive Your free gift of forgiveness. I need a Savior. Lord, I believe in You. Be my Lord and my Savior. Save me. I receive that now. Thank You Lord, for saving me. In Jesus' name. Amen."* —Creflo Dollar,

How Grace Teaches Humility Part 2—Sunday Service (YouTube)

Now go in peace. Stay in God's Word and truth. Strive to live in righteousness. There's kingdom work to be done. Go be about Your Father's business.

Jesus Loves You.

GOSPEL PLAYLIST

    These songs were in my playlist on heavy rotation through the years of me living through my stories at a young age up until the writing process of my testimonies for this book. I wish I could list them all but of course, I'm limited here or I'll be writing another book with just a list of songs. I'm sharing with you because these songs, in no particular order, gave me comfort while healing. May they bless you all the same.

1. God Is — Rev. James Cleveland
2. Open My Heart — Yolanda Adams
3. Uncloudy Day — Myrna Summers and Refreshing Springs
4. We Are Not Ashamed — Bebe & Cece Winans
5. Blessed and Highly Favored — Clark Sisters
6. Yahweh — Jokia
7. Can't Give Up Now — Mary Mary
8. Never Would Have Made It — Marvin Sapp
9. Jehovah Jireh — Jekalyn Carr

10. Jehovah Sabaoth — Donald Lawrence feat/Brittany Stewart
11. Returning — Joshua Rogers
12. More Than Anything — Lamar Campbell & Spirit Of Praise
13. Blessing Somebody Else (Dorothy's Song) — Kurt Carr & Various Singers
14. Over and Over — Trin-i-tee 5:7 feat/PJ Morton
15. Be Encouraged — William Becton & Friends
16. Redeemer — Karima
17. Lean On Me — Kirk Franklin/Various artists
18. Deliver Me — Donald Lawrence feat/Le'Andria Johnson
19. It Belongs To Me — Juan & Lisa Winans feat/Marvin Winans
20. Let It Rain — Bishop Paul S. Morton
21. Now Behold the Lamb — Tamela Mann
22. Jesus, I Love Calling Your Name- Shirley Caesar
23. I'm Available To You — Rev. Milton Brunson & The Thompson Community Choir
24. The Potter's House — Tramaine Hawkins
25. Jesus Is Love — Monifah feat/Boys Choir of Harlem
26. Safe In His Arms — Rev. Milton Brunson & The Thompson Community Choir
27. You Kept Me — Hezekiah Walker & LFT Church Choir

Gospel Playlist

28. Patiently Praising — Fred Jerkins feat/Lowell Pye
29. Stones — Kim Walker-Smith
30. We Fall Down — Donnie McClurkin
31. Excess Love Remix — JJ Hairston & Mercy Chinwo
32. Falling In Love With Jesus — Kirk Whalum feat/Jonathan Butler
33. Balm In Gilead — Karen Clark Sheard
34. Make Me Over — Tonex and The Peculiar People or Bri Babineaux
35. I Love You Lord Today — Benita Jones
36. He's My Rock — Bri Babineaux
37. Revival — Jules Juda feat/Tasha
38. Why We Sing — Kirk Franklin
39. Just Like God — Evvie McKinney
40. Optimistic — Sounds of Blackness (Not necessarily gospel but a message to keep your head to the sky/God. It was heavy on my rotation when I was in my early 20s, encouraged me, and gave me as much hope as any gospel song.)

DEVOTIONALS

DEVOTIONAL 1: OVERCOMING FEAR

Be strong and courageous. Do not be afraid or terrified because of them, for the LORD your God goes with you; he will never leave you nor forsake you. Deuteronomy 31:6

Fear can paralyze us but as believers, we have the assurance that we are not alone. We have a God who is always with us, guiding us, and protecting us. Let us choose to trust in His presence and His promises and step out in faith, knowing that He will help us overcome our fears.

DEVOTIONAL 2: OVERCOMING DOUBT

Jesus said to him, 'If you can believe, all things are possible to him who believes.' Mark 9:23

Doubt can be a hindrance to our faith, but we can overcome it by choosing to believe in the promises of God. Let us hold on to His Word and trust that He is faithful and true. As we believe, we will see His power and goodness at work in our lives, and our faith will be strengthened.

DEVOTIONAL 3: OVERCOMING TEMPTATION

No temptation has overtaken you except what is common to mankind. And God is faithful; he will not let you be tempted beyond what you can bear. But when you are tempted, he will also provide a way out so that you can endure it. 1 Corinthians 10:13

Temptation can be a powerful force in our lives, but we do not have to give in to it. As followers of Christ, we have been given the Holy Spirit to help us resist temptation and overcome sin. Let us trust in His strength and look to Him for the way of escape in every situation.

DEVOTIONAL 4: OVERCOMING DISCOURAGEMENT

Why, my soul, are you downcast? Why so disturbed within me? Put your hope in God, for I will yet praise him, my Savior and my God. Psalm 42:5

Discouragement can weigh us down, but we can overcome it by choosing to put our hope in God. Let us focus on His goodness and His promises and trust that He is working all things for our good. As we lift up our hearts in praise and worship, we will find renewed strength and joy in Him.

DEVOTIONAL 5: OVERCOMING HARDSHIP

I have told you these things, so that in me you may have peace. In this world you will have trouble. But take heart! I have overcome the world. John 16:33

Hardship is a part of life, but we do not have to face it alone. Jesus has overcome the world and as we put our faith in

Him, we can have peace in the midst of every trial. Let us look to Him for strength and comfort, and trust that He will bring us through every difficulty.

DEVOTIONAL 6: OVERCOMING PRIDE

Pride goes before destruction, a haughty spirit before a fall. Proverbs 16:18

Pride can be a stumbling block in our spiritual lives, but we can overcome it by choosing to humble ourselves before God. Let us acknowledge our need for His grace and His mercy, and seek to serve others with love and compassion. As we walk in humility, we will experience His favor and blessing in our lives.

DEVOTIONAL 7: THE ROLE OF SCRIPTURE

Your word is a lamp for my feet, a light on my path. Psalm 119:105

God's Word provides us with guidance and direction. When we are faced with difficult decisions, it is important to search the scriptures and seek God's guidance. As we meditate on His Word and allow it to guide our decisions, we can have confidence that we are making the right choices.

DEVOTIONAL 8: CONSIDERING THE CONSEQUENCES

The prudent see danger and take refuge, but the simple keep going and pay the penalty. Proverbs 22:3

Before making any decision, consider the potential consequences. By thinking through the possible outcomes, we can make wise choices that will lead to positive results.

DEVOTIONAL 9: TRUSTING IN GOD'S PROVISION

So do not worry, saying, 'What shall we eat?' or 'What shall we drink?' or 'What shall we wear?' For the pagans run after all these things, and your heavenly Father knows that you need them. But seek first his kingdom and his righteousness, and all these things will be given to you as well. Therefore do not worry about tomorrow, for tomorrow will worry about itself. Matthew 6:31-34

Trust that God will provide for our needs. As we seek His Kingdom and righteousness, we can have confidence that He will take care of us daily, as each day is our daily bread.

DEVOTIONAL 10: LEARNING FROM PAST MISTAKES

As a dog returns to its vomit, so fools repeat their folly. Proverbs 26:11

It is important to learn from our past mistakes and avoid making the same errors in the future. By reflecting on our past decisions, we can gain valuable insight and make better choices moving forward.

DEVOTIONAL 11: THE SOURCE OF WISDOM

If any of you lacks wisdom, you should ask God, who gives generously to all without finding fault, and it will be given to you. James 1:5

Making good decisions starts with seeking wisdom from God. He is the source of all wisdom, and He promises to give it generously to those who ask. Before making any decision, take time to seek God's guidance through prayer and studying His Word.

DEVOTIONAL 12: CONSIDER THE CONSEQUENCES

Let each of you look not only to his own interests, but also to the interests of others. Philippians 2:4

When making decisions, it's important to consider the potential consequences, not just for ourselves, but for others as well. Think about how your decision may impact those around you, and consider what is truly best for everyone involved.

DEVOTIONAL 13: SEEK WISE COUNSEL

Plans fail for lack of counsel, but with many advisers they succeed. Proverbs 15:22

Sometimes we need to seek the advice of others before making a decision. Surround yourself with wise and trusted individuals who can offer sound advice and guidance. However, ultimately, seek the guidance of the Holy Spirit as your primary counselor.

DEVOTIONAL 14: TRUST GOD'S SOVEREIGNTY

The heart of man plans his way, but the Lord establishes his steps. Proverbs 16:9

Ultimately, we must trust in God's sovereignty and His ability to work all things together for good. Even when we make mistakes, He can use them for His purposes. Trust in Him and His plan, knowing that He is in control.

DEVOTIONAL 15: KEEP A CLEAR CONSCIENCE

> *Cling to your faith in Christ, and keep your conscience clear.* 1 Timothy 1:19

Making good decisions requires keeping a clear conscience. Don't make decisions that go against your moral values, convictions, or what you know is right. Seek to live a life that honors God and aligns with His Word.

DEVOTIONAL 16: PRIORITIZE GOD'S WILL

> *But seek first his kingdom and his righteousness, and all these things will be given to you as well.* Matthew 6:33

Our primary goal in life should be to seek God's Will and to glorify Him. Prioritize His Will above your own desires and plans, and trust that His plans for you will ultimately be the desires of your heart.

DEVOTIONAL 17: CONSIDER LONG-TERM IMPACT

> *Do not be deceived: God cannot be mocked. A man reaps what he sows.* Galatians 6:7

Every decision we make has long-term consequences. Consider the long-term impact of your decisions, both for yourself and for others. Seek to make decisions that will bring about positive outcomes and honor God.

DEVOTIONAL 18: SURRENDER YOUR WILL

Not my will, but yours be done. Luke 22:42

Making good decisions requires surrendering our will to God's Will. Sometimes this means letting go of our own desires and plans in order to follow His path. Trust in His plan and surrender your will to Him.

DEVOTIONAL 19: LEARN FROM MISTAKES

And we know that in all things God works for the good of those who love him, who have been called according to his purpose. Romans 8:28

Perspective in life is key. If during the hard times we can remember we serve a God who loves us, fights for us, and is working even in what may be the worst of circumstances, we can push through with the hope we have in God that He will make it all work out for His glory and for our good.

DEVOTIONAL 20: THRIVING IN LIFE

I have come that they may have life, and have it to the full. John 10:10b

God desires for us to not only survive, but to thrive in this life. He has given us all that we need to live a life that is abundant and fruitful. But how do we go about thriving in life? Here are a few key principles:

1. Seek God's Will — To thrive in life, we must first seek God's Will for our lives. We were created with

a purpose and as we seek to fulfill that purpose, we will experience true fulfillment and joy. Spend time in prayer and in God's Word, seeking His direction for your life.
2. Develop a Positive Mindset — Our thoughts have a powerful impact on our lives. If we have a negative mindset, it can hold us back from thriving. Instead, choose to focus on the good things in your life and cultivate a positive outlook. Remember that God is always at work, and He can use even the difficult circumstances in our lives for our good.
3. Build Healthy Relationships — We were created for community, and thriving in life requires healthy relationships with others. Surround yourself with people who will encourage and support you, and invest in those relationships. Also, be willing to forgive and extend grace, as this will help to cultivate strong and healthy relationships.
4. Pursue Growth — To thrive in life, we must be willing to pursue growth in all areas. This includes spiritual, emotional, and physical growth. Set goals for yourself and work toward achieving them. Also, be willing to step out of your comfort zone and try new things, as this will help you to continue to grow and thrive.
5. Live with Purpose — Finally, to thrive in life, we must live with purpose. We were created to glorify God and make a difference in the world around us. As we live with purpose, we will find true meaning and fulfillment in our lives.

As we follow these principles, we will experience the abundant life that God has for us.

DEVOTIONAL 21: LOVE COMES FROM GOD

Dear friends, let us love one another, for love comes from God. Everyone who loves has been born of God and knows God. Whoever does not love does not know God, because God is love. 1 John 4:7-8

Love is not just an emotion. It is a characteristic of God Himself. As believers, we have the privilege of experiencing God's love and sharing it with others. Let us love one another as Christ has loved us.

DEVOTIONAL 22: LOVE IS PATIENT AND KIND

Love is patient, love is kind. It does not envy, it does not boast, it is not proud. It does not dishonor others, it is not self-seeking, it is not easily angered, it keeps no record of wrongs. Love does not delight in evil but rejoices with the truth. 1 Corinthians 13:4-6

The love described in 1 Corinthians 13 is the standard by which we should measure all love. Let us strive to love others with patience, kindness, humility, and forgiveness. Let us rejoice in truth and reject evil.

DEVOTIONAL 23: LOVE COVERS A MULTITUDE OF SINS

Above all, love each other deeply, because love covers over a multitude of sins. 1 Peter 4:8

Love is a powerful force that can cover our mistakes and shortcomings. When we love others deeply, we can forgive them for their mistakes and seek to restore broken relationships. Let us extend love and grace to others as we have received it from Christ.

DEVOTIONAL 24: LOVE YOUR NEIGHBOR AS YOURSELF

Love your neighbor as yourself. Mark 12:31

Loving our neighbors means treating them with the same care and concern that we have for ourselves. Let us seek to serve others, put their needs above our own, and show them the same love that Christ has shown to us.

DEVOTIONAL 25: LOVE NEVER FAILS

And now these three remain: faith, hope, and love. But the greatest of these is love. 1 Corinthians 13:13

Love is eternal and will never fail. When we love others, we are participating in something that will last forever. Let us prioritize love in our lives and relationships, knowing that it will endure for all eternity.

DEVOTIONAL 26: LOVE YOUR ENEMIES

But I tell you, love your enemies and pray for those who persecute you. Matthew 5:44

Loving our enemies goes against our natural instincts, but it is what Christ has called us to do. Let us show love and kindness to those who oppose us, trusting that God will use our actions for His purposes.

DEVOTIONAL 27: GOD'S LOVE FOR US

But God demonstrates his own love for us in this: While we were still sinners, Christ died for us. Romans 5:8

God's love for us is not based on our performance or worthiness. It is a gift that He has given us through His Son, Jesus Christ. Let us bask in His love and allow it to overflow into our relationships with others.

DEVOTIONAL 28: SALVATION THROUGH FAITH

For it is by grace you have been saved, through faith-- and this is not from yourselves, it is the gift of God--not by works, so that no one can boast. Ephesians 2:8-9

Grace is an undeserved favor, therefore salvation is a gift from God that cannot be earned through our own efforts. It is only through faith in Jesus Christ that we can be saved. Let us trust in His finished work on the cross and receive the free gift of salvation.

DEVOTIONAL 29: REPENTANCE AND SALVATION

Repent, then, and turn to God, so that your sins may be wiped out, that times of refreshing may come from the Lord. Acts 3:19

Repentance is a necessary step toward salvation. It is through confessing our sins and turning away from them that we can be forgiven and receive the gift of salvation. Let us humble ourselves before God and turn to Him for forgiveness and redemption.

DEVOTIONAL 30: SHARING THE GIFT OF SALVATION

> *Therefore go and make disciples of all nations, baptizing them in the name of the Father and of the Son and of the Holy Spirit, and teaching them to obey everything I have commanded you.* Matthew 28:19-20

As believers, we have the responsibility to share the gift of salvation with others. Let us be bold in proclaiming the gospel and inviting others to experience the same saving grace that we have received through faith in Jesus Christ.

THE GREAT COMMISSION

Then the eleven disciples went to Galilee, to the mountain where Jesus had told them to go. When they saw him, they worshiped him; but some doubted. Then Jesus came to them and said, "All authority in heaven and on earth has been given to me. Therefore go and make disciples of all nations, baptizing them in the name of the Father and of the Son and of the Holy Spirit, and teaching them to obey everything I have commanded you. And surely I am with you always, to the very end of the age." —Matthew 28:16-20 (NIV)

RESOURCES

TEEN HOMELESS HOTLINE

1-800-RUNAWAY

NATIONAL HUMAN TRAFFICKING HOTLINE

888-373-7888
SMS: Text HELP to 233733
Hours: 24 hours, 7 days a week
Languages: English, Spanish

NATIONAL DEPRESSION HELPLINE

Postpartum Depression (Consult your doctor if you have symptoms.)

866-629-4564

https://nationaldepressionhotline.org

It's a free, confidential, around-the-clock helpline for depression and/or anxiety. Call now for immediate assistance.

NATIONAL DOMESTIC VIOLENCE HOTLINE

1-800-799-7233
SMS: Text START to 88788
Hours: 24/7
Languages: English, Spanish, and 200+ through interpretation service

NATIONAL SEXUAL ASSAULT HOTLINE (RAPE CRISIS HOTLINE)

1-800-656-4673
Hours: 24 hours

988 SUICIDE AND CRISIS LIFELINE (SUICIDE PREVENTION HOTLINE)

988
SMS: 988
Hours: 24 hours
Languages: English, Spanish

AUTISM SPEAKS

1-888-AUTISM2 (1-888-288-4762)

www.austismspeaks.org

En Español: 1-888-772-9050

ayuda@autismspeaks.org

Resources

Consult a pediatrician if your child shows symptoms of Autism. Also, join national and local Autism groups on Facebook. They are not just for parents of children on the spectrum but family members as well, special needs teachers/therapists, or anyone in the community who wants to gain more knowledge.

SAMHSA NATIONAL HELPLINE

Alcohol/Drug Addiction Hotline (Also, join AA/NA and sobriety/recovery groups on Facebook.)

1-800-662-HELP (4357)

www.samhsa.gov

Christianbook.com

Lifeway.com

Lifewaywomen.com

www.bsfinternational.org

ABOUT THE AUTHOR

    Keka Samuels-Wilson is the daughter of a King, a wife residing in New Jersey, a mother of four, and a former LPN specializing in caring for severely ill children with disabilities. She also proudly serves as a Staff Sergeant in the U.S. Army. Her life is a testament to a higher calling, a divine purpose beyond herself.

    Born to fulfill God's plan, her mission transcends her individual existence. She is wholeheartedly dedicated to carrying out God's work, spreading the message of Christ's grace, and guiding others toward righteous living. Her continued presence on this earthly journey is a blessed gift.

    Drawing from her diverse life experiences, she founded Mikan Ministries. Each community and group that Mikan Ministries engages with holds a special place in her heart. These are encounters she has personally experienced during her life's journey. Her relatability makes Mikan Ministries more compassionate, beneficial, and vital in meeting the diverse needs of the people it serves.

    With a previous career in the broadcasting industry, she brings her knowledge and skills to the forefront in the form of Mikan Productions LLC. This media communications resource is poised to reach a wider audience, more communities, and the entire nation, further extending her impact and mission.